INTRODUCTION TO
BUSINESS

DANTES/DSST* Test Study Guide

© 2020 Breely Crush Publishing, LLC

DSST is a registered trademark of The Thomson Corporation and its affiliated companies, and does not endorse this book.

971010620143

Published by Breely Crush Publishing, LLC
10808 River Front Parkway
South Jordan, UT 84095
www.breelycrushpublishing.com

ISBN-10: 1-61433-671-7
ISBN-13: 978-1-61433-671-6

Printed and bound in the United States of America.

Table of Contents

Economic Issues

Economics is the study of how people choose to use limited resources to satisfy people's unlimited wants. Social responsibility is the idea that a business is part of something bigger than itself. It is part of a global community. With that knowledge comes the responsibility to do what is best for the company and for society as well. Some of the ways that companies can contribute to society are making environmentally friendly choices as well as contributing to charities.

There are four factors of production:

1. labor – the human resource, brain and brawn
2. land – includes all natural resources
3. capital – funds provided by investors and profits created
4. entrepreneurship – the processes of bringing the other factors together to create a good or service and a profit

Socialism is an economic system. Unlike capitalism, the government does the economic planning, owns most of the basic industries, controls the large industries and has a heavy tax to finance the welfare programs of the nation. Typical industries owned by a socialist government include coal mining, banking, major transportation like air, rail, etc. Some current social democracies include: Great Britain, Italy, Sweden, France and Austria. Under this system, the country supplies medical care, dental care, and college education.

Federal Reserve Bank

The Federal Reserve System in the U.S., often referred to as the Federal Reserve or simply "the Fed," is the central bank of the United States. It was created in 1913 by Congress to provide the nation with a safer, more flexible, and more stable monetary and financial system. Over the years, its role has evolved and expanded. The Federal Reserve's responsibilities fall into four general areas:

- Conducting the nation's monetary policy by influencing money and credit conditions in the economy in pursuit of full employment and stable prices

- Supervising and regulating banking institutions to promote the safety and soundness of the nation's banking and financial system and to protect the credit rights of consumers

- Maintaining the stability of the financial system and containing systemic risk that may arise in financial markets
- Providing certain financial services to the U.S. government, to the public, to financial institutions, and to foreign official institutions, including playing a major role in operating the nation's payments systems

Structure and Function of the Federal Reserve Banking Systems

There are 12 banks in the Federal Banking System, each located in a strategic area of the country. These regional Federal Reserve Banks share responsibility for supervising and regulating financial institutions and for providing banking services to depository institutions and to the federal government; and for ensuring that consumers receive adequate information and fair treatment in their relations with the banking system. The Fed's most important operational role is raising and lowering interest rates, creating money and using a few other tools to help stimulate or slow down the economy. This manipulation is aimed at maintaining low inflation, high employment rates, and targeted economic output. More on how the Fed actually manipulates the economy will be discussed in Section 3.

The Federal Reserve Bank is considered an *independent* central bank because its decisions do not have to be ratified by the President or anyone else in the executive or legislative branch of government. Moreover, the Fed does not receive funding from Congress, and the terms of the members of the Board of Governors can span multiple presidential and congressional terms; this supposedly precludes the possibility of a political appointee being put at the head of one of the most powerful financial institutions in the world. However, the Federal Reserve is subject to oversight by Congress, which periodically reviews its activities and can alter its responsibilities by statute. The main idea of keeping the bank as free from politics as possible is that the Central Bank wields considerable power to influence the economy and thus the socio-political state of the nation with ramifications for the rest of the world. For example, if an incumbent president wants to be re-elected, "convincing" (jawboning) the Central Bank to stimulate the economy might be good for the incumbent but eventually not for the country (spurring the potential for inflation). Responsibility for the proper management of a large part of the U.S. banking system along with controlling interest rates and money supply rests on the broad shoulders of the Federal Reserve Bank.

Ownership of the Fed

There exists some confusion on exactly who owns the Fed. It certainly sounds like a federal institution but such is not the case. Congress does have oversight of the Fed but the Fed is owned by member banks – which are privately owned. The Reserve Banks issue shares of stock to member banks. However, because of restrictions, owning stock in the Reserve Bank is quite different from owning stock in a private company. The

Reserve Banks are not operated for profit, and ownership of a certain amount of stock is, by law, a condition of membership in the Federal Reserve System. The stock of the Fed may not be sold, traded, or pledged as security for a loan; dividends are, by law, limited to 6 percent per year.

The Federal Reserve's income is derived primarily from the interest on U.S. government securities that it has acquired through open market operations. Other sources of income are the interest on foreign currency investments held by the System, fees received for services provided to depository institutions, such as check clearing, funds transfers, and automated clearinghouse operations; and interest on loans to depository institutions. After paying its expenses, the Federal Reserve turns the rest of its earnings over to the U.S. Treasury. Because of the protection of secrecy, the Fed is not required to file any sort of written financial report and nobody seems to know exactly what the real financial status of Fed operations are.

The President of the United States appoints the Chairman of the Fed for a four-year term which can be repeated without term limit. The chairman, along with the Federal Open Market Committee (FOMC), which is made up of other regional Fed bank presidents, oversees open market operations, the main tool used by the Federal Reserve to influence money market conditions and the growth of money and credit mainly through controlling interest rates and reserve requirements.

Basics of International Trade – Key Terms

Tariffs	Taxes on imports Increases cost of imported goods
Quotas	Limit on amount of specific import item
Subsidy	Government supports for an industry
Dumping	Sale of goods below market value
Trade Embargo	Ban on trade for political purpose
Trade Agreement	Establishes rules of trade; generally favorable
MFN Status	Nation receives all trade advantages other nations receive
Free Trade	Goods flow without government interference

Balance of Trade	Difference between value of imports and exports. Trade deficit/surplus
Exchange Rate	Value of one currency in terms of another

Economic Institutions

The economy is a technical and official name for the production, distributions for goods and services in exchange for other services or money. When someone creates a product they in turn market and sell that product to a customer. This is the most basic activity in the economy. Currency is the most common way to purchase goods and services. Although barter or trade still happens, most transactions are conducted with currency or credit.

Capitalism is a monetary and social system where individuals are encouraged to make new businesses and work for as great of a profit as they can. The United States is a capitalistic society. In a capitalistic society, the government has limited influence in private business although they do enforce some business laws and practices. **Adam Smith**, the economist is frequently referred to as the **Father of Capitalism**.

Socialism is a system where the good of the group supersedes the good of the private individual. Each person works for bettering society as whole. The government controls almost all natural resources, business and social programs.

In welfare capitalism, the government pays for all education and health coverage. It is a market based system as well. Sweden and Canada are examples of welfare capitalism.

Communism is when the means of production are owned equally and the profits are shared equally. Although it has been attempted many times to create a utopia of sorts based on communism, it is considered a flawed system. The book "Animal Farm" is a wonderful analogy to the social systems, particularly communism.

Globalization is the takeover and expansion of current markets into new global markets. For example, the cell phone market is still booming in the United States and has experienced great success in South America and other localities where the standard of living has been increased to allow for such products. Telecommunications are being added to the most rural of areas in South American and Africa. By searching out customers in these far places, companies are reaching new untapped markets of customers.

Two types of economic conditions are monopolies and oligopolies. In a monopoly, one business or company is the only place which sells or provides a particular product or service for which there is no substitute. Traditionally, monopolies are considered dangerous because it allows the business to charge whatever they wish for the product or service. For example, if there was only one gas station chain in the world, they could raise the prices on gas and people would have no choice but to pay.

Oligopolies are similar to monopolies, but different because instead of one business supplying the product, a few companies sell it, and because those few companies are so powerful, their policies influence and determine the actions of other business and each other. For example, think about the cell phone industry. Many large companies tend to buy each other out and merge, meaning that there are fewer and fewer companies. The ones that exist are quite large, with the small companies unable to keep up with the competition and go out of business.

The resource mobilization theory explains social movements as an attempt by people to join together in a rational manner to mobilize and obtain resources or reach goals. According to the resource mobilization theory, every social movement starts as an organization. That organization must then acquire support and resources, which it then uses in achieving goals. This theory applies to both political and economic situations.

 # *Theory and Practice of Management*

WHAT IS MANAGING ALL ABOUT?

In a broader sense, Management may be defined as working with people and groups of people with the sole intention of achieving organizational goals. From this definition you can see that the word "Management" is not tied down to managing business or industrial organizations. It has been given a broader perspective; Business, industry, educational institutions, political establishments, hospitals and nursing homes, churches and even families – come under its purview. People who manage should have interpersonal skills. Messrs. Paul Hersey and Kenneth Blanchard believe that "…the achievement of organizational objectives through leadership is Management…"

MANAGING – IS IT AN ART OR SCIENCE?

Managing is something which managers practice. They interact with people in an organization with a view to achieve organizational objectives. A Doctor practices medicine and an Accountant practices accountancy. They practice in their chosen fields because they have acquired skills. So, if we view managing as a practice, then it can be considered as an art. A science, however, needs systematic knowledge, crystal clear concepts, rational theories supported by experimentation and analysis. So, if we view management as a body of systematic knowledge, it can be considered as a science.

MANAGEMENT THEORIES

Management theories abound. In some way each theory has contributed a mite to the knowledge of management.

Theory	Its import in a nutshell
1. The Empirical or Case Approach	The experience of past situations to guide in the present. Find out why a particular action succeeded or failed by going deeper to analyze the basic reasons.
2. The Inter-personal behavior Approach	It is all about understanding people and their relationships. It mainly deals with the human aspect and stresses that if people understood other people perfectly, organizational goals could be achieved without much difficulty.
3. The Group-behavior Approach	In an organization people work not in isolation but in groups. The study of group behavior patterns is to know how groups affect production possibilities positively or negatively. It relates to the study of behavioral composition of groups, which are large, and how this impacts their relationships.
4. The Co-operative Social Systems Approach	As a corollary of the group behavior approach, the Co-operative Social System came into being. It deals with human relationship as a co-operative social system. Propounded by Christian Barnard, the essence of the co-operative social system is the co-operative interaction of thoughts, ideas, wants and desires of two or more people. His theory focuses on both interpersonal and group behavioral approaches and concludes that their interaction leads to a system of co-operation.

5. Socio-technical Systems Approach	Arising out of the co-operative social systems, another approach, mostly credited to E. L. Trist, seeks to emphasize the systems aspect of group behavior. It tries to relate group behavior with technical systems and those relationships. There should be a most harmonious relationship between groups of people (social systems) on the one hand and machines, systems and methods (technical system), on the other. It seeks to establish that personal behavior and group behavior are necessarily influenced by the technical system in which they work.
6. The Decision Theory Approach	This approach emphasizes that a Manager's most important function is Decision Making and therefore the decision should be the central focus. A manager goes ahead on the basis of evaluating innumerable alternatives and arriving at a most suitable decision, depending upon the facts and figures, and importantly, the extent to which he was delegated responsibility and authority. Since decision-making is the core, all the other functions of a manager are built around it, so say the decision theorists.
7. The Systems Approach	They view management as a system, which envelops within itself many subsystems, all operating within the total environment. A total unity, which is a collection interdependent of or interconnected with sub-systems working within a total environment. Concepts, ideas, thoughts, principles, theories or techniques (sub-system) in the area of managing (system).
8. The Mathematical or Management Science Approach	The Mathematical models form part of this theory. Each situation is considered in terms of available Mathematical models and then the situation is analyzed, arriving at a mathematically correct decision.

9. The Contingency or Situational Approach Professor. J. Lorsch of Harvard University was one of the founders of this theory.	It tells us that any manager's performance is directly related to a set of given circumstances or contingencies. Some theorists also feel that it takes into account not only situations but also the behavior pattern of an organization. The drawback is that instead of promoting total organizational loyalty, it encourages departmental loyalty.
10. The Managerial Roles Approach	This is the latest approach propounded by Professor Henry Mintzberg, to observe what managers do and using such observations as a platform for analyzing and concluding on the basis of such analysis, what their roles (i.e., activities) are. This approach has visibility. The Professor studied the roles of many Chief Executives and concluded that they not only perform the classical function of a Manager, such as planning, organizing, coordinating, leading and controlling, but also perform a variety of other functions as well.
11. The Operational Approach	This approach believes in imparting knowledge from every other field of knowledge such as sociology, Mathematics, Economics, Psychology, etc., which fits simply into Management

Scientific management, or Taylorism, is a management style created by Frederick Taylor. Scientific management is basically like the assembly line system. Prior to Taylor, most products were created by individual skilled artisans. For example, one person (or specialized group) would be responsible for assembling an entire car or lawn mower or creating an entire piece of software. Under scientific management the process is broken into smaller units, requiring less knowledge and making the process more efficient. For example, instead of one person designing a computer game, one person may be responsible for graphics, another for underlying code, a third for sound effects and so on. Frederick Taylor is known as the father of scientific management.

The Impact of External Environment

Every organization has to operate under different external environments. It is within the environment and therefore has to be responsive.

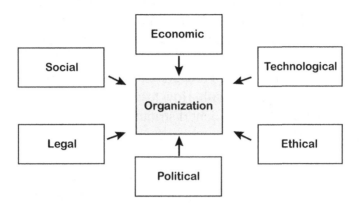

The operations of any organization whether domestic or international depend largely on these externals, which act as a constraining influence. In an international organization the impact of external influences is even more rigorous. A person deputed from a parent country to a host country has to be knowledgeable about the host country's economical, political, legal, educational, social and cultural environment.

Additionally, the management of an international company has to spend a lot of time in determining the orientation of management best suited to the host country. A birds-eye view of Management Orientation is represented by:

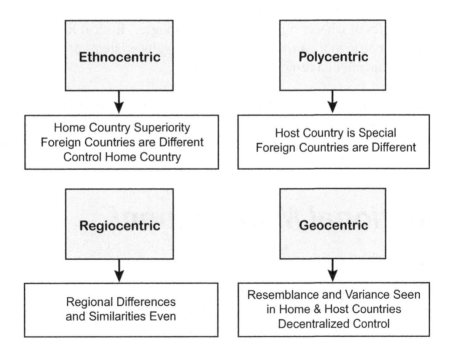

Economic Environment: Deals with the availability of capital, rate of interest, labor availability and how well they are organized, general price levels, the degree of productivity, the willingness of entrepreneurs and availability of Managerial skills.

Technological Environment: How good the available knowledge is used through technology is a factor to reckon with. How to conceive ideas, how to design, how to produce optimally, how to effect efficient distribution and how well marketing is done, are all questions that are technology-oriented.

Social Environment: This is the value systems unique to a particular group of people or society. The value system consists of attitudes, behavioral pattern, needs, wants, expectations, levels of education, the degree of intelligence, general beliefs, customs and traditions followed by a particular group of people or society.

Political and Legal Environment: This consists mainly of laws, rules, regulations, governmental policies, etc., that directly affect an organization. Managers are to act within the laws of the land, follow the rules and regulations faithfully, and in case of a change in policy that has a direct bearing on the enterprise, to act accordingly.

Ethical Environment: Longman Advanced American Dictionary describes (1) "Ethics" and (2) "Ethical" as: (1) "…the study of the moral rules and principles of behavior in society, and how they influence the choices people make…," and, (2) "…relating to principles of what is right and what is wrong…" Ethical Environment therefore means holding on to moral principles, guided by value systems prevalent in society and generally behaving in a responsible way.

Social Responsibilities: Organizations as well as managers should be socially responsive to the society as a whole and should be able to do their bit when a situation calls for it. They should be seen as contributing members of solutions to the social problems.

 # Functional Management

PLANNING

Planning comprises of setting objectives i.e., goals for the organization as well as developing work-maps that identify the ways and means of achieving such objectives. It is the most basic function of managing and all other functions are built, brick by brick, over it. Broadly speaking it revolves around the selection of not only the total organizational objectives, but departmental, even sectional goals, and more importantly spelling out in clear terms the ways through which such objectives, goals are to be accomplished. What? How? When and Who? are decided in advance at the planning stage. What to do, How to do, When to do and Who exactly will do is the primary objective of good planning. It, therefore, precedes all other managerial functions. Since planning and controlling are related most intricately they become inseparable and therefore, a good plan always spells out yardsticks for accomplishing the planned objective. It is obvious control measures are also part and parcel of a well thought out plan.

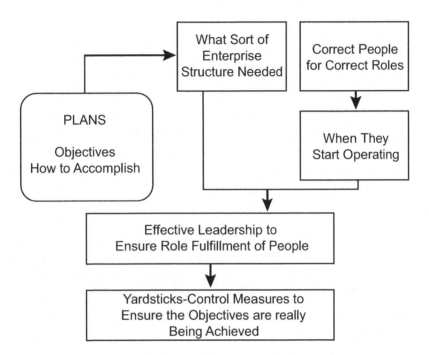

TYPES OF PLANS

- **Mission Statement**: What is the main purpose of the company? The purpose of a University is primarily teaching and then doing research on studies. Every organization's principal planning document gives its mission statement explaining what the organization stands for and what its activities are going to be. Example: The mission statement of DuPont has been spelled out as "...better living through chemistry..."

- **Objectives**: Objectives are identified goals of an organization towards accomplishment of which all organizational activities are directed. It is an action program specifying what should be achieved over a specified time and what resources are to be employed in achieving such objectives. What is an organization going to do in terms of business, i.e., what business it is aiming at and how it is going about it? What is the time frame, what are the resources and where from they are coming, who all are going to be responsible and who all are accountable for achieving the spelled out objectives? These points are to be clearly considered.

- **Policies**: A policy can be defined as a predetermined action course that serves as a guide for the identified and accepted objectives and goals. A policy indicates the management strategy towards attainment of the overall objectives and goals and seeks to establish a platform of guiding principles, which makes delegation of work to lower levels easy.

- **Procedures and Rules**: They can be defined as guides to action. In order to handle future activities one needs a plan that shows clearly what methods are to be used. And this plan that establishes such methods is known as procedure. Procedures are available at every level of an organization. This method is more widely adhered to in the lower levels. Some organizations have even departmental procedures cogently spelled out for the people of the department to follow. Rules give us distinct action plans without permitting any sort of discretion whatsoever. The action plan may spell out what action or non-action is to be taken in clear terms. They are very simple plans.

- **Programs**: Programs contain a simple, complicated or complex plan of activities developed primarily for carrying out stated policies. It simplifies the process of decision-making. A program generally consists of objectives, policies, procedures, rules, individual task allocations, what action or inaction to be taken or not taken by whom and when, and what resources are to be employed in order to successfully carry out a specified goal. Programs are also assisted by appropriate budgets in quantity or dollar terms.

- **Budgets**: Budgets are statements of targeted results reduced to quantifiable terms. An operating budget is a "profit plan." A territory budget spells out what the target is for the territory in terms of dollars and what will be the total resources to be spent in order to achieve that quantified (in dollar terms) target. A budget is seen as a tool of control. If an organization has variable output levels, they normally have flexible/variable budgets.

STEPS IN PLANNING

1. Analysis of Opportunities: Thorough knowledge of the plus points of your company and the products, market knowledge, knowledge on competition and knowledge as to what exactly the needs and aspirations of the customer are in so far as the products are concerned.

2. Setting of Objectives: An unambiguous objective that spells out clearly where the organization is at the moment and why, where it should be heading, what should

be the best direction to get there, what specific action should be taken by whom and when, and what measures should be watched to get information on whether the plan is going on the right track and at the right speed.

3. To identify the basis: The plan has to work in what sort of environment – both external and internal. To take note of all factors that form part of the external environment.

4. To identify, analyze, compare and choose the best of available alternatives.

5. To design relevant plans that are supportive in nature such as purchasing capital goods, purchasing materials, sub-assemblies and components, recruiting, training and placing needed personnel, etc.

6. Quantify for control: reduce your actions into numbers – in other words work out budgets. Example: volume of business both in quantity and dollar terms for the targeted period, inventory, operating expenses, expenditure on capital goods, sales territory budgets, etc.

There are long term plans such as a 10 year or a 5 year plan which reflects the continuity of policy and short term plans like an annual plan that sets targets for the year to be achieved and which, for the sake of control, is further bifurcated into half yearly, quarterly and even monthly plans.

DECISION MAKING

The central pith, the core of planning is decision making. There are alternatives available. Choosing the best alternative from a plethora of available alternatives and sticking to it is the focus of decision-making.

In decision-making you have to identify the Limiting Factor, which can be defined as something that stands in the way of achieving a goal. The impediment. Identify the limiting factor or factors and solve them in order to arrive at the best possible decision. How to evaluate alternatives? There are Marginal Analysis Models and Cost-effective Analysis Models. The Marginal Analysis deals in analyzing the additional units of revenue one gets from incurring a certain unit of additional costs. The cost-effective analysis deals in cost-benefit analysis, i.e., the ratio of benefits to costs. Your experience, ability to experiment and an analytical bent of mind helps you to arrive at a rational decision under specific given circumstances. Operations Research lends a scientific aura to management decision-making. There are goals, models, variables, limitations – all such factors are built into quantifiable mathematical terms or formulae to decipher and arrive at the best decision possible under a given circumstance. Not all the managers are equipped mathematically to decide among alternative solutions. It is sometimes difficult to quantify a factor. In such cases operations research can do little about it.

There is <u>Risk Analysis</u>, which again is a method steeped in mathematical terms – it tells you what probabilities are there to arrive at decisional outcomes. There are <u>Decision Trees</u>, which again are statistical models which tell us which are the possible decision points, chance events which are likely to occur and what probabilities are there for each course of action. Then there is Preference Theory, which tells you a given manager's willingness to take or refrain from taking (unwillingness) risks.

CHANGE

Change is the essence of life. There are different levels of changes.

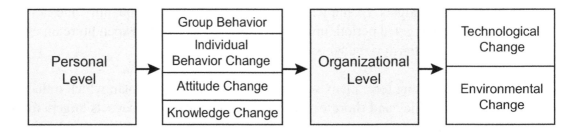

At the personal level knowledge changes are the easiest to make. Once you read this book you will have gained a little more knowledge than you had before starting it. Attitudinal change is not as difficult as individual behavior change, though time and conscious effort is needed. Group behavior change is a little more difficult than individual behavior change. Group behavior change affects an organization. If people as a group within an organization demand certain things, say, increased rest periods, lesser number of work hours, it impacts the organization and the Personnel Manager has to deal with such a situation. At the organizational level, environmental changes – Social, Economic, Political, Legal – any changes in any of the components, are going to affect the organization adversely. In the case of technological change, an organization has to face the music if it does not adapt itself to the changes adeptly and with speed. A change is certainly a limiting factor in the planning process. Rapid changes more especially in the environmental and technological areas impact organizational plans adversely. In the field of computers, the chip capacity of the hard disks increased in breathtaking speed. A 2-Gigabyte hard disk is considered obsolete – as there are 40 and 80 GB hard disks available. Again, the increase in speed of chips is breathtaking! Once radios used bulky, noisy, inelegant, vacuum tubes, which became obsolete after Bell laboratories designed transistors! In such rapidly changing, highly competitive environment, it is your own creativity and techniques bordering on innovation that are necessary to exist. Fast adaptability to change is the key.

ORGANIZING

Organizing defines organizational roles to be played by individuals, their positions and the authority relationships. Every role should be clearly defined with distinct objectives in mind. The major duties to be performed by individuals, how responsibilities are to be delegated and with what authority are all definitions to be included in the organizing process. Should also indicate what resources are available, and what information and tools are necessary to carry out such roles effectively. This is organizing in a nutshell.

A formal organization is what we have seen above. An informal organization according to Chester Barnard is any joint personal activity without conscious joint purpose, even though possibly contributing to joint results. The relationships in an informal organization never reflect in any organizational chart. There may be sub-assembly groups, stress groups or accounts groups, i.e., groups of individuals. However, each group identifies itself as a contributing member and acts in unison where the group's ideal or any given member's identity or right is challenged.

ORGANIZATIONAL THEORIES

Many theorists propounded a number of theories of which the following 3 are important:

(1) Classical Organization Theory
(2) The Mechanistic Theory
(3) The System Theory.

The Classical Organizational Theory deals in specializing job assignments, works towards easy managerial functions, seeks to establish authority structures and delegation of responsibility and authority, maintains bureaucracy which speaks of offices and roles, and institutes formal channels of communication among members of different departments in the organization. It deals in division of labor, vertical and horizontal specialization, scalar authority, etc.

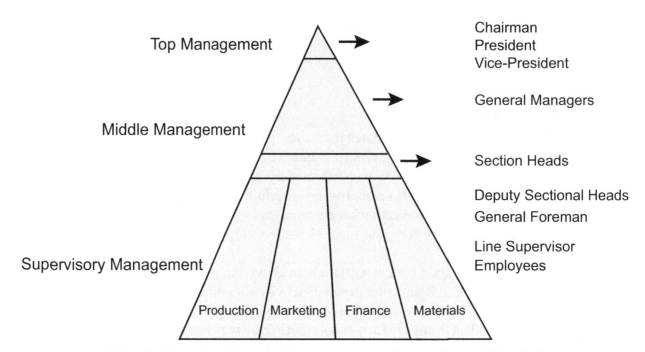

VERTICAL AND HORIZONTAL SPECIALIZATION

The Mechanistic Theory states that organizational change is inevitable and that organizations and people within the organizations have no other choice except following natural law. Industrialization brought in its wake a laissez faire philosophy in political circles, which advocated the integrity or virtue of letting the natural process take its own course. This theory was supported by economic philosophy prevalent at that time. In a way it is a precursor to the later scientific management movement. The theorists had foreseen the potency of competition. They thought specialization was a tool for obtaining competitive advantage. The later versions of this theory harp on compensation structures. Both the classical organizational and the Mechanistic theories took people for granted. This gradually created uncertainties in the minds of workers and opposition started. This situation necessitated bringing focus on people. Unions and collective bargaining were begun. Human relations principles were born out of necessity. Approximately 30% of the U.S. workforce is unionized.

The Systems Theory deals with interdependence instead of independence of variables and their interactions. It started with a more intensive, very broad, wide-angle – involving a number of variables to measure complex inter-relationships – and inclusive viewpoint. Group behavior is seen in the system as broadly shaped and influenced. There are various elements in an organizational system but the common choice of an element is the individual in an organization. It identifies the system as changing, evolving and most dynamic. The systems model recognizes the environment of the system and other related variables, which includes all other subsystems, and seeks to elucidate an adequate explanation of organizational behavior. The system as a whole is seen as an open system.

ORGANIZATIONAL STRUCTURES

Any formal organization can be described as an intentional structure of roles. For the sake of functionality, a formal organizational structure is divided into many departments on the basis of their functions. There may be an Accounts department, a Marketing department, a Production department, a Material department, an Engineering department and so on. A department typically has a Head or Boss followed by a Deputy and then the assisting employees. In such a scenario, the roles of the Department Head, the Deputy and the assisting employees should be very clear and the authority relationship should be spelled out. The cooperation of all the people making up a department should be effective in order to achieve the overall organizational objectives. How many people can a department head or his deputy effectively control is the crux of the "Span" of management. There are two types – (1) Narrow Span, and (2) Wide Span.

Structure
An Organization with a Narrow Span

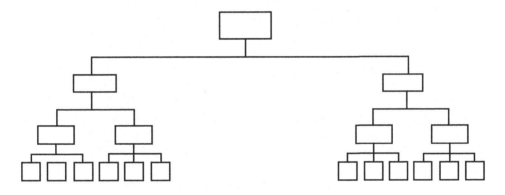

Structure
An Organization with a Wide Span

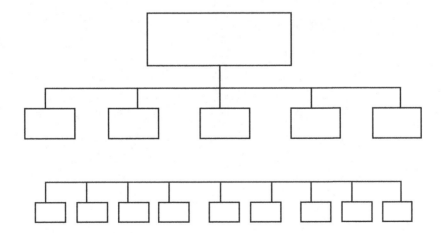

In a narrow span organizational structure, close supervision is possible, good control, and communication between Department Head and subordinates occur quickly. The disadvantage is that the super is closely involved in the subordinate's work – delegation is missing. There are many levels of management necessitating increased cost to the organization.

In a broad span organizational structure delegation becomes essential. There is a possibility of a superior losing control of subordinates. Managerial effectiveness dictates placing high quality managers. Delegation of responsibility along with requisite authority is the crux of broad span organizational structure.

AUTHORITY

In order to achieve company objectives and to sail smoothly on the chosen direction towards that objective, the superiors need authority to enforce compliance of company policies, procedures and rules by subordinates. 'Scalar' authority is identified with rank, position, as well as title.

LINE AND STAFF AUTHORITY

They are identified with relationships and not departments. In Line Authority a superior is directly responsible for the organizational actions of a subordinate. It entails making decisions and acting upon them. Staff Authority is limited only to the extent of giving counsel/advice. The advice given by Staff Authority is not binding on Line Authority.

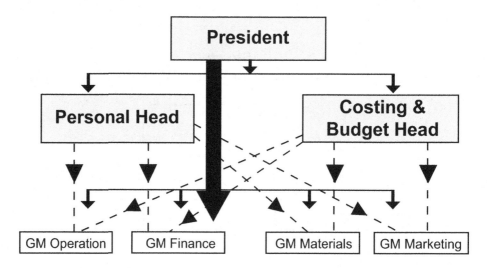

LINE AND FUNCTIONAL AUTHORITY

Functional Authority is the right of people in other departments (i.e., other than one's own) to control selected policies, practices, procedures, processes or other functional matters with the sole aim of accomplishing set organizational goals.

DELEGATION OF AUTHORITY

The idea behind delegation is to make organizing easy. A collective effort is the key to success in an organization. Delegation of Authority happens when a super-ordinate bestows on a subordinate discretion to make decisions in the best interest of the organization. It can be specific to perform a task or a cluster of tasks, or general, written or unwritten. It is also possible for the super-ordinate to revoke the delegated authority any time.

UNITY OF COMMAND

The reporting relationship of a subordinate will be smooth and effective if it is to a single superior. If an employee has to report to more than one superior then confusion, inefficiency, lack of control and total chaos prevail. A subordinate reporting to a single superior is unity of command in its simplest definition.

CENTRALIZATION AND DECENTRALIZATION

In centralization all authority is concentrated at the top. In decentralization, decision making is widely dispersed. A decentralized authority, if it is re-centralized or to put it simply, if all the authority dispersed is revoked and centralized again, it is called Re-centralization of authority.

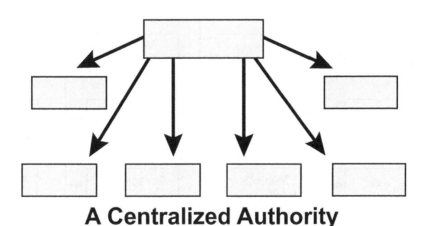

A Centralized Authority

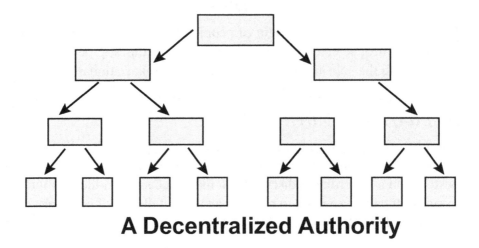

A Decentralized Authority

ORGANIZATION CHARTS

Functional grouping of a manufacturing organization:

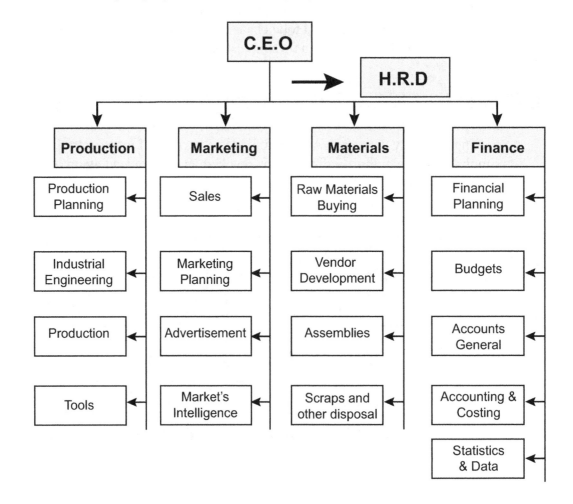

Territorial grouping of a manufacturing organization:

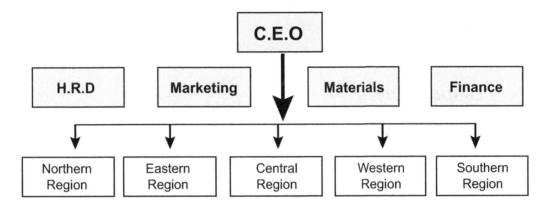

Market-oriented grouping of an organization:

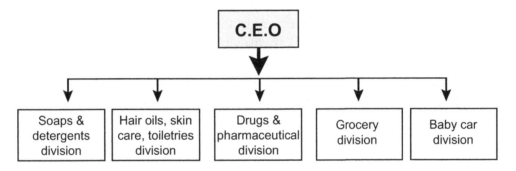

STAFFING

In organizing we have seen authority structures, broad departmentalization, delegation, etc. In other words we have a structure and we need people to fill up the structures to do meaningful jobs. Staffing, therefore, is a systematic and methodical filling up of positions in an organizational structure by identifying total manpower requirements, recruitment, selection, placement, appraisal, promotion, training and compensation. Organizing and staffing are closely linked.

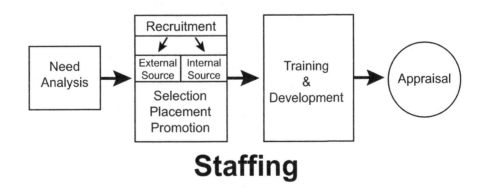

Staffing

DIRECTING

Directing = Leadership + Motivation + Communication. Directing is the process that seeks to influence people towards spontaneous and willing accomplishment of overall organizational objectives. Let us consider the components of Directing.

LEADERSHIP

Peter F. Drucker, the Modern Management philosopher and guru states in his book "The Practice of Management" "…The successful organization has one major attribute that sets it apart from unsuccessful organizations: dynamic and effective leadership…" Again, George R. Terry, in his wonderful book "Principles of Management" points out that: "…Of every one hundred new business establishments started, approximately fifty, or one half, go out of business within two years. By the end of five years, only one third of the original one hundred will still be in business…" Almost all the failures were attributed to <u>ineffective leadership</u>. This tells us in clear and unambiguous terms all about leadership. In other words, the core of leadership is accomplishment of goals <u>with</u> and <u>through</u> people. Every leader has a style. The style of leaders is the consistent behavior patterns that they exhibit when they seek to influence people in order to accomplish organizational goals. The style is the consistent perception of the followers/ subordinates of the leader and not the leader's perception itself.

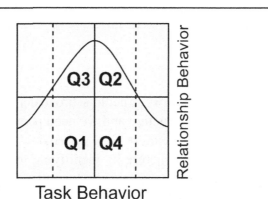

Q = Quadrant

Q1 = Telling stage where the leader perceives the subordinates maturity level as immature. Here he spells out clearly every task.

Q2 = Selling stage where the leader perceives the maturity level of his subordinates as moderate. Here he just gives what is expected and he would like the task done.

Q3 = Participating stage where the leader perceives the subordinate to be fairly matured and invites him to participate in decisions.

Q4 = Delegating stage were the leader thinks that the subordinate to be fully matured to take on responsibilities. He only gives a broad outline and leaves the execution to the subordinate.

There are despotic leaders who only demand what they want normally in high decibels, and encourage no initiative. They are task leaders. On the other side of the spectrum you have leaders who value human relationships, who are polite but firm with subordinates, encourage initiative and are willing to share responsibilities.

Many leaders **empower** their employees by allowing them to make their own decisions and/or giving them authorization to do certain behaviors to help a customer.

MOTIVATION

William James of Harvard University conducted research on Motivation. His findings are noteworthy. He found that hourly employees whose work pattern he studied could hold on to their jobs, if they performed at 20 to 30% of their ability. His studies further elucidated that workmen can work up to 80 to 90% of their ability if they are highly motivated! In other words if the employees are highly motivated their work ability jumps from 20-30% to 80-90%!

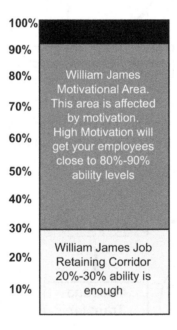

For some money can be a good motivator. For some others safety, i.e., security, job-satisfaction, congenial atmosphere, social needs, esteem needs and self-actualization needs are important. Challenge in one's job is a motivation for some people. Rewards for accomplishments are also a motivator.

Gainsharing and profit sharing are two ways that companies can motivate their employees to be more efficient and effective workers. With profit sharing, a company will specify a certain amount of profits that go to employees in the form of bonuses or stock options. Therefore, an employee's compensation will be directly tied with how profitable the company is and they will have incentives to work harder. With gainsharing, the idea is to motivate the employees to work more efficiently so that costs are reduced. For example, if employees get work done in half the time, the company's wage expenses are cut in half and their profitability increases. With Gainsharing, companies will allocate an amount of the money that is saved from increased profitability and share that with the employees.

COMMUNICATION

In communication there is a sender and a receiver. If the sender sends information (message) to the receiver and if the information is understood in full by the receiver, you have communicated successfully. The main purpose of communication in an organizational setting is to influence action aimed at achieving the common goals of the organization.

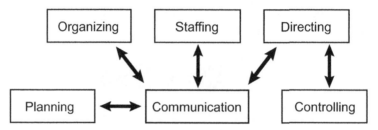

Communication is a very important factor in effective leadership and management. Not only the leaders (superiors) but also the followers (subordinates) should be adept in communicating.

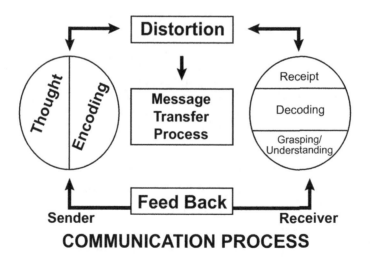

COMMUNICATION PROCESS

In an organization there are upward and downward communication, horizontal communication and diagonal communication.

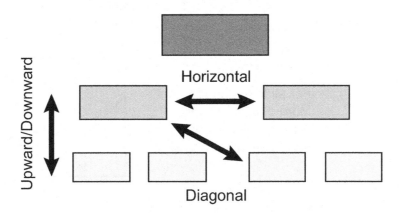

Communication/information flow in an organizational setting

Communication can be oral, written or non-verbal. When a message is repeated through various media, the comprehension and recall of that message is high with the receiver of such message. Simple words, using personal pronouns, adding graphs or graphics, short sentenced paragraphs, logical, cohesive and cogent presentation, and avoiding verborrhea will ensure good communication.

GROUP DYNAMICS

This is one of the training techniques used in organizations. Group dynamics works with role playing coupled with simulation which seeks to emphasize group behavior, how groups influence decision making and how inter-group rivalry or conflicts affect organizational effectiveness. Participants discuss team development, team member hygiene, issues that are construed as disruptive and team health.

PROBLEM SOLVING

Of all the skills a manager is expected to possess, analytical and problem solving abilities are most important. There are broadly three skills associated with managing. They are (1) Conceptual skills, (2) Human relation skills and (3) Technical skills.

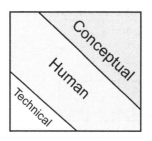

For Top Management Less technical, more conceptual and a good deal of human skills

For Middle Management More of technical and conceptual skills and a good deal of human skills

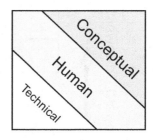

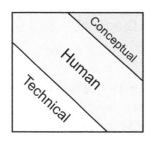

Supervisory Management More of technical, less of conceptual skills and a good deal of human skills

(Originally developed by Robert L. Katz
in Harvard Business Review - 1955)

For all the levels – Top, Middle and Supervisory, the emphasis is Human skills. "…I will pay more for the ability to deal with people than any other ability under the sun…" said John D. Rockefeller, one of the great American entrepreneurs. Managers should be ever vigilant to identify problems as they arise, analyze and track the core issue and then solve the problem by addressing the core issue and exploiting the opportunities present. Opportunities are always present in every possible threat.

CONFLICT RESOLUTION

Ask yourself, what is the conflict all about? What are the causes of the conflict? What are the possible solutions? And, what is the best of the possible solutions? Is the solution acceptable to all? Yes means you have resolved the conflict.

In an organizational backdrop, if the individual and group goals are seen as close to the organizational goals, there is bound to be an integration of goals, which satisfies all concerned.

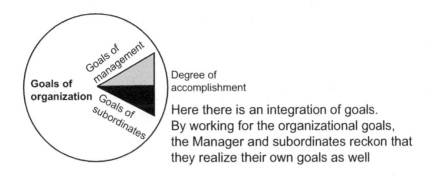

Here there is an integration of goals.
By working for the organizational goals,
the Manager and subordinates reckon that
they realize their own goals as well

In psychological terms conflict arises when frustration develops. The blocking or stymieing of goal accomplishment is known as frustration. In an organization conflicts arise mainly because the people in the organization have not understood their roles, assignments, tasks as well as those of their co-workers. You can educate people by having proper organization charts, authority structures, clear-cut job descriptions and job specifications, together with specific goals. Job enrichment and job rotation are also helpful

CONTROLLING

In every organization, the top management sets out the overall company objectives, departmental targets, etc., for the managers and their team of people to accomplish during a given period of time. Managers use many tools to ensure the targeted objectives are realized effectively and efficiently. Controlling, in its larger perspective, involves the measurement of activities of subordinates in order to know whether the organizational targets are realized as per plans and if there happens to be a lagging behind, what corrective actions are to be taken to ensure 100% achievement. There are 4 elements in a control system:

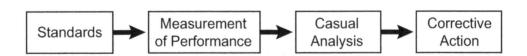

MANAGEMENT BY OBJECTIVES – MBO

Introduced by Peter F. Drucker (The Practice of Management) and popularized by Messrs George Odiorne and John Humbe, this participative approach is good for goal setting as well as control. The superior and the subordinates of an organization jointly identify its common goals – this is the first step. Then they define each individual team member's major areas of responsibility, which is considered on the basis of results, expected of the individual – this is the second step. And using these measures as a sort of guide to run the organization as well as appraising each individual team member's contribution – this is the third step.

NORMAL STANDARDS IN PRACTICE

Standards fall within the following types: 1) Physical Standards, 2) Capital Standards, 3) Revenue Standards, 4) Cost Standards, 5) Intangible Standards, and 6) Goals standardized for verification.

Physical Standards: Quantified standards at the operating level. Products produced in numbers, in value, material used in weightage and value, labor employed in house and in value, services rendered in value, etc.

Capital Standards: Physical items and monetary value pertaining to the capital goods used in production.

Revenue Standards: Giving monetary values to realized sales.

Cost Standards: Monetary value for the cost of operations, such as machine-hour-costs, cost of material per unit, cost of labor per unit, cost per unit of sales, etc.

Intangible Standards: These relate to human efforts and for these, it is difficult to allot a standardized measurement value.

BUDGETS – AN IMPORTANT CONTROL TECHNIQUE

Budgets are plans for a specific future period of time given in numerical or value terms. They are anticipated results in value terms of a given plan. There are cash budgets, revenue/expense budgets, materials budgets, products budgets, capital expenditure budgets, etc.

MANAGERIAL CONTROL TOOLS (MILESTONE BUDGETS)

Gantt Charts: There are many types of Gantt charts in vogue. They may be called a particular type of bar chart and the measuring unit invariably is time. For example, a progress chart – here the planned target is compared with the actual accomplishment:

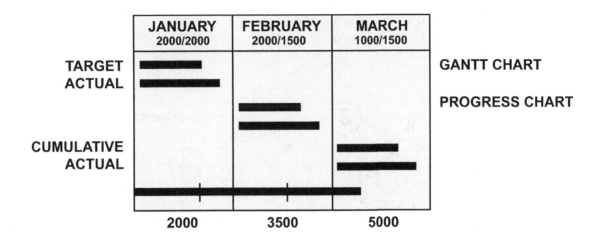

Means Chart: This is used in statistical quality control situations.

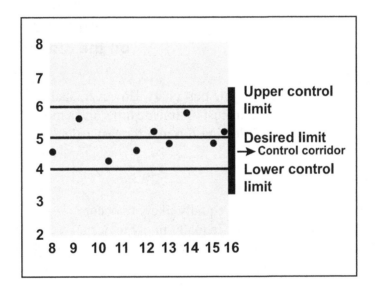

Pert (Program evaluation and review technique) and CPM (Critical Path Method):

NASA used these techniques extensively in its space programs. A project's most probable time of completion can be worked out through these techniques. Let us see an organization's budget preparation in Pert form:

Job	Description	Time Required
a	Forecasting sales	10 days
a	Market research on pricing structures of competitor	4 days
b	Sales valuing	4 days

c	Production schedules	6 days
d	Costing of production	5 days
e	Budget preparation	8 days

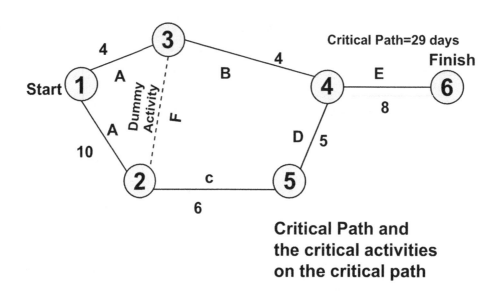

**Critical Path and
the critical activities
on the critical path**

The above is a very simple pert chart. However, such charts are prepared by giving a most pessimistic time, a most optimistic time, and a most probable time. These can then be reduced into the following formula for easy calculation.

Weightage:

t_o = optimistic time – equally likely to occur
t_p = pessimistic time – equally likely to occur
$4t_m$ = most probable time = 4 times more likely to occur than t_o, t_p.
t_e = time expected

Formula: $t_e = t_o + 4t_m + t_p / 6$

You have to arrive at standard deviation $S_t = t_p - t_o / 6$, which is one sixth of the difference between two extreme time estimates. Since standard deviation is the square root of any given distribution, we calculate variance from $V_t = (t_p - t_o / 0)2$ using probability distribution, and thus we can say expected duration of a project.

A dummy job takes only zero time for performance but it is used to show the precedence relationship. Critical path may be defined as the longest path in the network. Jobs (activities) throughout the critical paths are known as critical jobs, or critical activities.

Small Business, Entrepreneurship, Forms of Business and Franchise

It's the great American dream to open and run your own business. This dream is coming true for many Americans through their own ideas, purchasing a business or purchasing a franchise.

A sole proprietorship is when you own a business yourself. You have a great deal of responsibility like with any business but you carry a lot of personal risk as well. The debts of the business are also considered to be your debts. For example, if you are a sole proprietor of a restaurant and you decide to close the business while still having debts, you are personally responsible to pay those debts. If you fail to do so, creditors can sue to seize your property, like your house.

A general partnership is when a business is owned between two or more people. Like a sole proprietorship, the partners are liable for all business debts. The partnership is dissolved when one partner dies or withdraws.

A joint venture is created with a specific project in mind. This partnership dissolves when completed.

A limited partnership is made up of general partners and limited partners. General partners take care of the day-to-day running of the business while limited partners only contribute capital. The legal ramifications are different for each type of partner. The limited liability partner only risks his initial capital investment while the general partner has full legal liability.

A limited liability partnership (LLP) is created to protect partners from liability caused by other partners. An LLP is more informal than a corporation and receives partnership tax treatment.

Limited liability companies (LLC) are popular because they give you both the limited liability of a corporation and the favorable taxation of a partnership. An LLC is a separate legal entity so no member has personal liability.

A corporation is a separate legal entity. It may also be known as a C corporation. This business must be set-up with the state, usually with the help of an attorney. A corporation is owned by shareholders. It is also managed by the board of directors. Because some of the work involved in a corporation can be time consuming and administrative, including annual meetings, issuing stock, taking minutes, etc., many individuals elect to have these duties handled by professionals.

An "S" corporation is when an individual's tax returns show income generated or losses accrued by the corporation. Converting to an "S" corporation affects the tax status but does not generally effect the legal protection offered by the corporation.

Doing Business As or DBA is a way to have a fictitious name for your company or any other name than your company name.

A franchise is a commercial relationship between an individual or group and the owner of a trademark. For example, many large fast food chains do not actually operate most of their locations. Rather, they are franchises. Individuals pay them various monthly or annual fees (called royalties) in exchange for allowing them to use their name, logos and advertising. This way the companies are able to expand faster and increase profits without the hassle of worrying about day to day operations of individual stores. Reverse royalties would be when the owners of a trademark pay individuals to use their name (instead of the other way around).

A franchise is a ready-made business that you can purchase. You pay franchise fees, annual fees as well as a portion of your profits to the franchise. Besides all that money, you must conform to their way of doing business. While this can seem like a great way to start a business, once you get your feet wet in running the business day-to-day there will be items you want to add to your store or a different way you want to see things done. With a franchise, most of the time, that won't be possible.

Part of a franchise is brand integrity. If you walk into a McDonalds in Alaska, you should get the same menu of the McDonalds in California with the same "great taste." That's what makes a franchise good, you can rely on quality. BUT this is only great for the customer. Franchise fees can be very expensive, most in the range of $100,000 and up for most businesses, and that is just for the right to have the franchise. Add to that supply costs, building and labor costs and your total capital outlay is very expensive. When you come down to it, purchasing a franchise is just purchasing yourself a job, but a job where you have to work twice as hard to make money. You are better off opening your own business from scratch or investing in other ventures. Other examples of franchise businesses are Subway, Pizza Hut, and Jiffy Lube.

The SBA or Small Business Administration was created in 1953. This government agency not only counsels new business owners but can help get loans, find locations for a new business and help with many other business issues. The SBA does not itself grant loans, but rather it backs them. This way, small businesses can get backed by the SBA and get a loan from a bank that the SBA partners with, making it easier than if they had to find the loans themselves. The SBA was created under President Eisenhower with the intent of protecting the needs of small businesses.

 Business Ethics

Although there may once have been a day when a simple handshake could be considered to ensure a business transaction, business today requires far more monitoring and regulating. The study of business ethics is an attempt to apply moral principles to business operations. Ethics is closely associated with the term morality. Often the two terms are interchangeable, however there is a distinction. Morality is used to describe a person's character. It encompasses their beliefs about behaviors and can dictate how they act or respond in different situations. With morality, the focus tends to be on individuals. Ethics is the study of morality. It focuses on societal acceptance of and adherence to moral principles. Ethics focuses on the social structures which morals are a part of. Ethical principles can be considered generally accepted guidelines or expectations about the way that people (or businesses) behave.

There are three major categories of ethics, all of which come into play in the everyday operations of businesses. Three different schools of ethics are social ethics, economical ethics and legal ethics. Social ethics have to do with the way people interact with one another.

For example, the morality of lying to or stealing from another person falls under social ethics. Economic ethics have to do with business and money related issues. For example, whether or not an American company with overseas offices or factories should have to abide by United States labor laws would fall under economic ethics.

Legal ethics has to do with the actions of lawyers. Things such as lawyer-client privilege fall under legal ethics. For example, one aspect of legal ethics is noisy withdrawals. A noisy withdrawal is when a lawyer becomes aware of frauds committed by their client and withdraws legal representation for their client. They then notify the proper authorities of what they know. For example, in cases involving the SEC, if a lawyer becomes aware of fraud or illegal activities by their client they should remove themselves and notify the SEC of the wrongdoing.

However, determining ethical principles that businesses should follow is not necessarily as straightforward as it sounds. This is because businesses thrive on the ability to generate a profit. Consider, for example, a grocery store. The store purchases the groceries from a supplier. In order to make a profit the grocery store must sell the groceries for more than they paid for them. At face value this may seem "wrong" of the company to do, they are knowingly overcharging all of their customers.

However, if they didn't then there would be no grocery stores and people would have to purchase groceries from the suppliers themselves – a much more difficult process in the end. Therefore, the perceived overcharging which could be considered unethical, truly benefits everyone involved. Of course, this is a simplified example, and not all business practices can be considered in these terms, nor do they have eventual benefits, but it serves to illustrate the point that ethics is not always a cut and dry situation. What it comes down to is that business ethics is a study of the extent to which an action can be viewed as necessary for businesses to thrive, and when it becomes entirely unethical.

The Federal Trade Commission Act was passed in 1914 and, in addition to creating the Federal Trade Commission, it dictated that advertising cannot be deceptive or unfair, and it must be backed up by evidence. This policy of honest advertising is referred to as truth in advertising.

Many scandals in the early 2000s served to increase the number of federal regulations involving business, and lowered people's trust in the business community as a whole. These scandals included well known people and companies, including Enron, Tyco International, Martha Stewart, Nike and Worldcom.

Enron was created in 1985 by the merging of two large gas pipeline companies. By 2000 it had become one of the largest companies in the United States, generating over $100 billion in revenues. Not surprisingly it came as a shock when just a year later (In 2001) the company declared bankruptcy, costing shareholders and investors billions. Under further investigation it was shown that the company had been using accounting practices that were not accurate and showed the company's financial situation in better light than it was by hiding its debt. This was done by creating legal entities called special-purpose entities (SPEs) and then having them assume the debt. This created the impression that Enron had more assets than it did, and that there was a healthy cash flow because the SPEs did not appear on the balance sheet.

Another company associated with accounting scandal is Tyco International. By the end of 2000, Tyco International was a major company, bringing in around 30 billion dollars. The company had three main divisions, involving fire protection, electronics and packaging. When Dennis Kozlowski became the company's Chief Executive Officer (CEO) in the early 1990s he proceeded to expand the business into other industries, and the company soon became one of the largest producers of medical equipment as well.

However, when the SEC launched an investigation of the company, it was discovered that Kozlowski had stolen millions from the company. As one example, he had purchased nearly 20 million dollars of art for himself and used company funds to pay for the art, and the taxes on it. He also threw an extravagant party for his wife using company funds. In total, it was determined that he had stolen around 75 million dollars. In addition, Kozlowski along with the company's Chief Financial Officer, Mark Schwartz, had arranged to have 7.5 million shares of stock (worth 450 billion dollars) sold without authorization, and then moved the money out of the company and into their own accounts. When the deceit came to light, Tyco International's stock prices dropped by 80%.

The scandals continued as another company, Worldcom, was forced to declare bankruptcy when an internal audit revealed billions of dollars of wrongly reported expenses. The company had been reporting operating expenses as investments. In total, the company had misreported over three billion dollars of expenses as investments. Correcting the financial statements showed that instead of growing, as it had appeared, the company was actually shrinking and in debt. Stock prices fell 99%, once again to the loss of shareholders in addition to over 15,000 people who lost their jobs.

These three incidents shook the securities markets as shareholders lost billions of dollars. The underhanded accounting practices of the three companies resulted in a widespread loss of confidence in the securities market. As a result of this loss of faith, the **Sarbanes-Oxley Act** was passed in 2002. The Sarbanes-Oxley Act tightened laws enforcing accounting and auditing practices with the intent of restoring stakeholder confidence in securities markets.

Another scandal involved Martha Stewart. Stewart built her company from a small gourmet food shop and catering business to founding Martha Stewart Living Omnimedia in 1996. She had become the iconic symbol of a homemaker and the company soon owned multiple magazines, TV programs, books and a newspaper and radio column. However, in 2001 she came under investigation for insider trading. Insider trading occurs when a person trades stock when they have information not available to the general public which influences their actions.

In Martha Stewart's case, the stock in question was ImClone stock, a pharmaceutical company for which her friend, Sam Waksal, was an executive. The day before Im-Clone's stock value plummeted because it was not given FDA approval for a new drug, Stewart sold off nearly a quarter million dollars of shares, along with Waksal, who sold off nearly five million dollars of shares. Both were eventually convicted of insider trading and Stewart was sentenced to five months in prison and five months under home arrest for her involvement. Insider trading, along with accounting practices, is an aspect considered under business ethics.

The Nike scandal started when it was discovered that the famous athletics brand was producing many of their products in Asian factories with low wages and dangerous working conditions that would not be acceptable in the United States. The company was soon barraged with complaints, and protests were held outside of many of their stores. Within two years their revenue and stock prices had been cut in half. As a result, the company began an exhaustive public relations campaign. They accepted responsibility for the working conditions in foreign factories, and began to work with the factory owners to improve them. They established work codes, and outlined steps to achieving them. In addition, the company went around the country to different universities to restore their image in the eyes of college students.

This scandal raises many questions about business ethics. For example, should United States based companies have to adhere to United States laws even when operating in foreign countries? Also, if so, should this be universally true – or extend only to certain laws? How should child labor, safety codes and wages be addressed? Should the United States based company be held responsible for factory conditions, even if they do not own the factory that supplies their products (as was the case with Nike)? The list goes on, and all of the questions are ones that business ethics seeks to address. However, in many cases there is still not a satisfactory compromise.

Despite the many scandals of the past few decades, the evidence that better ethics actual helps businesses has become increasingly accepted. For example, some of the benefits of doing business ethically are that employees have an increased feeling of loyalty to the company. When employees feel that their company is essentially "good" they are more likely to want to continue working there. A track record of good ethics also increases loyalty from investors. If a company is doing reasonably well, and the investors feel that they can trust the company to be ethical in their practices, they feel more secure in investing in the company.

On the other hand, unethical practices (as shown through the examples above) typically result in downfall of stock prices and loss of profit for the company. By extension, good ethics is therefore healthy for a company's profit. When given the choice between an ethical company and an unethical company, people are more likely to purchase from a company they consider ethical. Consider the example of Nike. Their revenues fell by 50% and people were protesting in front of their stores when they felt like the company was being unethical. Practicing good business ethics has become a way for companies to give themselves a competitive advantage over other companies in their respective industries.

On the large scale, business ethics is also important, but not all ethical problems in business occur between one business and another business or between business and the public as a whole. Some ethical issues apply to the proceedings within business, and these issues also come under the scrutiny of business ethics. For example, issues of conflict of interest, sexual harassment, nondisclosure agreements and discrimination are all addressed by the field of business ethics as well.

ETHICS REGARDING WHISTLEBLOWERS

There are numerous laws and regulations which are designed to encourage and protect whistleblowers (those who "snitch" or report of their employers misdeeds to the authorities or the media). For example, the Whistleblower Protection Act. This act protects employees of the federal government who expose incidences of waste of funds, abuse of authority, violations of laws or any other issue from any action being taken against them. If an employee feels that they are being retaliated against in some way, then they may file a complaint and have the issue taken care of.

Another protection developed for whistleblowers is the False Claims Act. The False Claims Act works from the opposite end of the Whistleblower Protection Act and encourages employees to expose efforts by companies to avoid paying federal taxes, providing false information to the federal government, conspiring to do either of those things or other acts which involve fraud towards the federal government. The act allows for compensation to the whistleblower of between 15 and 30 percent of the amount recovered as a result of their informing.

A third act with implications for whistleblowers is the Sarbanes-Oxley Act. The act has four elements relating to whistleblowers. The first is that a company must have a system of internal auditing through which an employee can file complaints. The second is that the act creates a legal responsibility for lawyers to inform on clients who are in violation of SEC regulations. The third is that the act prohibited any form of retaliation by employers to employees who legally inform about ethics violations to the proper sources, and provided the whistleblower with compensation for any legal fees. The fourth element of the act is that it allows for violators of any of the other elements can be charged under criminal law.

Financial Management

Financial management is an important part of any manager's job. It's important to understand how your department contributes to the bottom line and you need to be able to understand that impact through finance.

Debt financing is the use of borrowed funds. Equity financing is the provision of funds by the owners of the business. This could include the company issuing stock to raise capital or through depreciation. Depreciation is an expense item that is deducted from revenue although it does not immediately need an outlay of cash. Maturity is the amount of time until a debt must be paid. Leverage is when you use borrowed money to earn more money than the amount of interest paid on the funds. For example, any business owner can use the concept of leverage. If a baker borrows $1000 to buy a new stove that will allow him to make more money than the $1000+interest, he is using leverage.

Deregulation is the reducing or elimination of laws regarding how an industry does business. A good example would be most of the utilities in the U.S.

Working capital is a firm's investment in their assets. An example would be the baker's over.

What are other examples of assets a company could have?

- Equipment

- Capital (money)

- Accounts Receivables (invoices out to customers for work that has been completed)

- Inventory

- Prepaid expenses (such as a year of pre-paid medical insurance)

New working capital is current assets minus liabilities. What are some examples of liabilities?

- Accounts Payable

- Notes Payable

- Payroll

- Outstanding vacation hours/pay

Liquidity is a company's ability to make payments that are due. If the baker needs to pay his employees $1500 and only has $1600 in the bank, he is not very liquid. Liquid can also refer to the ease of transferring other assets such as inventory into ready cash.

Short term fund sources generally come from these areas:

1. Trade Credit. For example, when the baker buys flour from his supplier and doesn't pay until he's sold his bread – no bank is involved, just the supplier and the baker.

2. Factoring. This is when a business sells its accounts receivables to a financial institution at a discount. The baker sells bread to a supermarket and is owed $2000. To get cash quickly to pay for upcoming expenses and payroll, the baker could sell this invoice to a bank or individual for $1800. This means that the baker gets $1800 today and the factor (a.k.a. the bank or person who just bought the accounts receivables) has to get the supermarket to pay. The factor will get $200 for his trouble, which is usually not much hassle.

3. Commercial Bank Loans. This is a standard loan from a bank.

4. Line of Credit. This is a credit agreement with a bank to pay it off in a short period of time. Another form of a line of credit would be a revolving credit where the borrower could pay it off over a period of time while accruing interest. Credit cards are revolving credit accounts.

Promissory note is a written promise by a customer to pay a sum of money and interest to the supplier or payee at a certain date.

A certified check is a check certified by a bank to have funds backing the check. This guarantees that the check will not bounce. A cashier's check is very much like a certified check with the exception that the bank is the guarantor of the funds on the check, where a certified check is on an individual's account.

Treasury Bills are a government obligation which matures in 91, 182 or 365 days. Treasure Notes are a government obligation which matures between 1-7 years. Treasure Bonds are a government obligation which matures in a specified period of time over 7 years.

Merger is the act of joining two companies. Acquisition is the purchase of another company. Venture capitalist is a person or an organization that invests money in a company for a part of the profits.

Securities

The securities market is basically the buying and selling of stocks and bonds. A stock split is when a company gives each shareholder more shares. If you own 500 shares of eBay and they have a stock split, you will now have 1000 shares. A cash dividend is a payment to shareholders. A stock dividend is when that payment is paid in stock instead of cash.

Over-the-counter market is a network of dealers that trade unlisted securities. A new company that is preparing to go public or have its IPO, Initial Public Offering, must first reveal certain business details to via prospectus to the SEC or Securities Exchange Commission.

Speculative trading is the buying and selling of securities in hope of near-term changes in pricing. Sometimes investors do not pay for their stock right away. They are allowed to borrow part of the money from their broker. Margin is the price that must be paid in cash.

Short selling is a strategy you can use if stock prices are falling. Short selling involves selling shares you don't own to a buyer. A put option is an option to sell a specific stock at a specific price and time in the futures. A call option is an option to buy a stock at a specific price and time in the future.

An index fund is a mutual fund made up of a group of stocks that mimic the S&P 500. The S & P stands for Standard and Poor's.

Par value is the price that is actually stated on the stock and in the company records. However, stock is rarely sold at par value and the par value has no influence on the price at which it sells. The price at which the stock is actually bought and sold is referred to as the market value.

Another important value to understand is the price earnings ratio (or P/E ratio). The P/E ratio describes the relation between the market price per share of a stock and the Earnings Per Share (EPS). The EPS is the net income of the company for each piece of stock that is circulation (basically the earning for each owner or stockholder). Based on the company's net income, the Board of Directors may choose to issue dividends. If they issues dividends, for each piece of stock a person owns, they will receive a specified amount of money taken from the company's profits.

Occasionally if a company wishes to make their stock more marketable, such as if the price has gotten too high and people aren't trading it as frequently, they will do what is called a stock split. When this happens, each stock in circulation is split into two stocks worth half the value. This way the stock price goes down but the owners still hold the same value and the same share in the company. The added benefit is that the stock is easier to trade.

Different types of stock have different advantages and disadvantages. The most basic and well known form of stock is called common stock. Buying common stock is the equivalent of purchasing a small portion of a company. The owner has the right to vote on matters affecting the company, and has a right to dividends (if the Board of Directors decides that they will distribute dividends). However, if a company goes bankrupt, the holders of common stock are the last people to receive their money. Also, the price of common stock is volatile and subject to fluctuations.

Another type of stock is preferred stock. Preferred stock is considered senior to common stock, meaning that it is higher ranked. This is because preferred stock carries less risk than common stock does. Typically preferred stock, while still fairly low on the list (beneath both outstanding debts and bonds), is above common stock if a company goes bankrupt. Preferred stock also guarantees dividends over a certain period of time. However, owners of common stock do not usually have voting rights and can expect a lower return over time than with common stock.

In addition to stocks, a person can also invest in bonds. When a person purchases stock they are purchasing ownership, or equity, in a company. When a person buys a bond they are purchasing a creditor stake in the company. Buying a bond is basically like loaning the company money. Holders of bonds are guaranteed to receive interest payments, called coupon payments, and are guaranteed to get their money back when the bond's term is up (when it comes to maturity). Bonds are considered senior to either type of stock and holders of bonds are paid before stock holders if the company goes bankrupt.

Risk Management

There are four ways to deal with risk:

1. Assuming the risk – setting aside enough money to pay for potential losses
2. Minimizing the risk – screening employees, network passwords, etc.
3. Avoiding the risk – avoiding certain industries (i.e., lumberjacking)
4. Shifting the risk – purchasing insurance policies

Computer Hardware and Hardware Functions

The term computer **hardware** refers to any of the electronic components that make up the computer such as the monitor, the CPU, the disk drives, or the printer. Hardware is separate from **software**, which is the general term for any program that performs calculations and controls what you see on the monitor. A computer comes with some basic software when it is purchased; this software is known as the operating system. An **operating system (OS)** is a master control program that oversees all the functions of the computer and manages the way in which information is placed onto the various hardware devices. Microsoft Windows is an example of a popular operating system.

The computer's **CPU** or **central processing unit** is the main microprocessor that controls the computer. Most personal computers (PC's) are powered by microprocessors that are manufactured by Intel, such as a Pentium or Celeron processor. The speed of the CPU determines how quickly software programs will perform their functions. There are three components to a CPU: the arithmetic logic unit, a control unit, and a set of registers.

Every computer has an **instruction set**, which is a list of keywords that corresponds to all of the operations that the CPU contains. A CPU can be a **complex instruction set computer (CISC)** that supports approximately 100 instructions for greater speed or a **reduced instruction set computer (RISC)** with a minimal set of instructions designed for a specialized application. **Registers** are specialized storage areas that store values while the instructions operate upon them. The **arithmetic logic unit (ALU)** is the component of the CPU that supports the standard arithmetic functions like add and subtract as well as logical operations like AND and OR. The **control unit** is the electronic controller over the operations that the instructions perform much like the brain controls our actions.

Computer Devices

Another critical hardware device is the **hard disk** or disk drive. The hard disk is an electronic component of the computer that is used for storing information and may also be called a **hard drive**.

Main memory is another name for a computer's RAM or Random Access Memory. Main memory is memory which is internal to the computer (whereas flash drives or discs are external memory sources). Main memory is directly connected to the CPU which allows it to be accessed and executed more quickly than any other type of memory. However, main memory is also volatile, meaning that it is emptied when the computer is turned off. Because people want programs that they are using to run quickly, the computer will copy information into the RAM so that the things a user is currently working on are easily accessed when it is needed and then discarded later (this is why things must be saved to the hard drive which is not main memory because it does retain information).

Moore's law is based on an observation made by Gordon Moore in 1965. He showed that since the invention of the integrated circuit, the number of transistors per square inch, or the data density, had approximately doubled every year. Moore's law is his prediction that this trend would continue. Because in recent years the trend has slowed slightly, the current definition of Moore's law is that the data density will double every 18 months.

The hard disk is an integral part of the computer and is portable only to the extent that the computer itself is portable, such a notebook or laptop PC. Alternate drives are available to handle portable information storage devices such as **floppy disks, diskettes** or **CD**'s. Floppy disks are portable storage devices that are 5.25 inches and mostly out-of-date today while diskettes are 3.5 inches wide and are encased in plastic. CD's or **compact disks** are the latest in portable information devices. All of the storage devices can be divided into **files**, which represent individual documents or other collections of information that are identified by unique names.

One medium that can be used to store information is a Compact Disc-Recordable, or CD-R. CD-Rs are small flat discs composed of a polycarbonate plastic layer, a thin metal sheet, a layer of polymer dye on which information is recorded and a protective coating. The CD-R technology is a Write Once Read Many (WORM) technology. This means that information can only be stored on the disc once, and cannot be removed or rewritten, but it can be viewed as many times as needed. One of the benefits of using CD-Rs is that they are relatively cheap, easy to obtain and convenient to store because they are portable. Also, one of the primary improvements over other storage discs such as CD-ROMs is that CD-Rs can be written from a home computer. However, they store only up to 80 minutes worth of data and wear out fairly quickly. These are not to be confused with CD-RW which can be re-written.

One form of data storage is through a Compact Disc Read Only Memory, better known as CD-ROM. CD-ROMs are composed of a polycarbonate plastic under layer, one or more thin metal layers and a lacquer coating for protection. CD-ROMs have the ability to store at most 100 minutes of data, or about 300,000 pages of text. They are often used by software distributors because it allows programs to be used without allowing them to be modified. CD-ROMs support both sounds and graphics. Like CD-Rs, CD-ROMs are easily obtained and stored. However, they also cannot be rewritten or erased.

The computer user communicates with the software and CPU by entering information through a **keyboard**, which is called an **input device** because it is used to enter information into the computer. The keyboard provides alphabetic, numeric, punctuation, symbols and control keys. When a key is depressed, an electronic signal that is unique to the key is sent to the CPU. The operating system typically displays the associated letter, number or symbol on the **monitor**, which is a piece of hardware that resembles a television screen. The computer user also enters information by using a communication device known as a **mouse.** A mouse is another input device. This device fits easily in the human hand and is designed to roll on a flat surface that roughly translates to the monitor's area. The mouse is used to locate an area on the monitor that the user is interested in. Clicking the buttons on the mouse is a typical method for selecting options that are displayed on the monitor by software programs.

The keyboard, monitor and mouse are the primary peripheral devices that are used for entering information into the computer. A **peripheral device** is any electronic component that is attached to the computer but external to it. Another external peripheral device is a **scanner**, which is used to copy paper documents or pictures into memory on the hard drive. A touch screen is another input device that is used in applications that are available to a general user. The **touch screen** enters the user's choices based upon a simple pressing of the indicated area of the pressure-sensitive panel. **Bar code readers** are used in business applications to interpret bar codes that indicate what the product is; bar code readers are particularly important in warehousing applications. A **point-of-sale (POS) terminal** is a computerized cash register that allows the input of data such as item sold, price, and method of payment. A **GUI or graphical user interface** is primarily how most people use computers today. Instead of typing in commands and codes into DOS, we click on pictures (graphics) as representations of files, hence the name.

Digital cameras can now be connected directly to a personal computer for downloading pictures onto the hard disk.

Just as there are a variety of peripheral devices for input, there are also numerous **output devices,** that is, components whose main purpose is to retrieve processed information that is stored in the computer's memory. The most familiar output device is a **printer**, which produces a paper copy of the desired document, picture, or graphs. Some printers are now special purpose devices that are designed only to print pictures. The computer **monitor** serves as an output device when it is used to retrieve information that is stored in memory. The **PC speakers** are also an output device for audio messages that accompany software systems or that are recorded on Internet web sites.

Computer Configurations

A **personal computer (PC)** is a small computer that is equipped with its own operating system and peripheral devices that are needed typically by one individual. PC's are differentiated from a **personal digital assistant (PDA)**, which is a hand-held computer that is customized for everyday functions for personal organization, such as an appointment calendar, an address book, a notepad and fax or other two-way messaging capability.

Large companies historically have relied upon some form of mainframe computer to handle their voluminous data processing needs. A **mainframe computer** is a multi-user computer capable of simultaneously processing thousands of calculations. Mainframe computers were the primary type of computers available from the 1960's onward.

DIGITAL REPRESENTATION

Computers are electronic and can only store information as a group of **binary digits** that is composed of 0's and 1's only. Each binary digit is known as a **bit.** Eight consecutive bits in computer memory are called a **byte.**

Our normal arithmetic is base 10 or decimal, with digits 0-9 only. Binary arithmetic within the computer is base 2, with digits 0-1 only. So decimal 0 is 0 binary, 1 is 1, but 2 is 10 binary, and 3 is 11 binary, 4 is 100 binary as so on. While the internal computer performs **numeric calculations** in binary, the operating system converts the internal binary to the decimal system we are accustomed to whenever the numbers are sent to an output device such as the monitor or printer. Sometimes very large numbers are stored in the computer in a form known as **binary-coded decimal (BCD)** where each decimal digit is stored as a 4-bit binary number.

How are letters or text stored? The letters that come in as electronic signals from the keyboard are converted to **Extended Binary Coded Decimal Interchange Code (EBCDIC)** for IBM mainframe computers and **American Standard Code for Information Interchange (ASCII)** for personal computers. The basic idea for these codes is that every letter of the alphabet and every other symbol, like the punctuation marks and percent sign, are converted to a binary code that fits into an 8-bit byte; however, ACSII coding uses only 7 of the 8 bits. These byte-oriented encoding schemes can handle 256 possible characters and symbols and thus are not suited for languages that have more symbols, like some of the Oriental languages.

Pictures have their own graphics digital representation or **Joint Photographic Experts Group (JPEG)** format. This format can represent up to 16.7 million color variations for each **pixel** or picture element. A pixel is the smallest picture element that an output device can handle. A picture is composed of a grid of pixels. Another picture format is **Tagged Image File Format (TIFF)** that is used for scanned photographic images. Graphs and graphics files are compressed using **Graphics Interchange Format (GIF)**. Video has its own format as well, namely the **Moving Picture Experts Group (MPEG)** format which provides for the compression of digitized videos and animation.

 Accounting

Financial accounting is being able to determine exactly where a business is at financially based on their sales, income and expenses. We already know what assets and liabilities are from a few pages back. Now let's learn the basic accounting equation: Assets – Liabilities = Owner's equity (capital).

A balance sheet is a financial statement that shows the assets (left) and the liabilities (on the right). Here is an example:

Assets	Liabilities & Stockholder's Equity
Cash	Accounts Payable
Accounts Receivable	Accrued Wages
Inventory	Estimated Tax Liabilities
Prepaid Expenses	Bonds Payable
Land	Capital Stock
Building	Retained Earnings
Less accumulated depreciation	
Intangible assets (patents)	

A fixed asset is an asset held longer than one year. Intangible assets have no physical form – they can include patents, trade secrets, etc.

The income statement is created with the following formula:

Revenues – Expenses = Net Income

Gross profit is the difference between net sales and cost of goods sold.

The standards which dictate the **financial statements** which businesses much produce require that businesses account for the revenues and expenses which they incur. However, the recording of revenues and expenses do not necessarily have to coincide with the collecting or paying of cash. For example, if a company sells goods on account, they must state the revenue because they sold the goods, but they will not collect the cash from the revenue until some specified time in the future. Because of this, it is often useful for companies to compile a statement of cash flows so that they can track the inflows and outflows of cash to ensure that they have sufficient cash on hand to conduct business day to day and month to month.

Financial statements are important because they allow for comparability between companies and aid in keeping companies honest which protects investors. It is important that there are measures in place to ensure that financial statements are collected accurately. These measures are referred to as internal controls. Internal control involves assessing and evaluating the integrity of financial statements, and instituting policies and safeguards to protect against possible problems. Some examples of internal controls include hiring independent auditors to review financial statements, dividing up duties so that no single employee has the ability to manipulate financial statements, requiring proper authorization for employee's actions and other measures.

Although there are many regulations which dictate how financial statements should be collected and presented, there are still many assumptions which are made in collecting them, and it is always possible for companies or individuals to be dishonest. Because of this, is it important that companies hire independent auditors to go through financial statements and determine whether they are reasonable and accurate. Because auditors are not actual employees of the company they can give an unbiased opinion of the company, and can see possible problems. It is the job of an auditor to evaluate and assess financial statements, and certify that they are reliable.

Liquidity refers to the ability of an asset to be converted into cash. For example, a business sells its inventory, at least in part, on a daily basis. Because of this, inventory is considered to be liquid because it is quickly converted to cash. On the other hand, things such as homes tend to be less liquid because it takes time and work to sell and convert them into cash. Because of this, a business may have a lot of wealth and assets, but have problems making payments on loans and debts because the money is tied up in land or investments. This would be considered a liquidity problem. The more liquid a company is, the better able it is to pay off its debts, and therefore the more stable it will be.

All companies borrow money at some point, and the question that they have to decide is whether to seek **short term** or **long term financing**. Short term financing is useful for short term situations. Some examples of short term financing include short term loans and trade credit (buying inventory on account from suppliers). It is often easier to obtain and has a lower total cost than long term financing.

A business could use short term financing if they have cash flow problems. In this case, they would just need some extra cash until their money from sales came in, so the need would be short term. If a business is incurring temporary or short term costs they may also consider short term financing. For example, an accounting firm will have a lot of extra work during tax season and may hire temporary employees. They could use short term financing to pay them.

Long term financing, on the other hand, is useful for long term problems. Sources of long term financing are equity financing (selling stocks and bonds) and long term loans from banks. Long term financing has lasting impacts on the company, but can be necessary and useful. Long term financing would be used to fund major projects. For example, if a small family owned hotel wished to expand into a large chain they would use long term financing. Long term financing is also used in funding the procurement of fixed capital such as new machines for which the expense is incurred only once.

When a business purchases something on account, the annual savings rate on that purchase can be determined by finding the savings for that purchase, and multiplying it by the number of purchase periods in a year. For example, on a 2/10, net 30 term the savings would be 2%. The number of 30 day periods in a year is approximately 12. Therefore the annual savings rate is 2% times 12 or approximately 24%.

Specific Identification and the Need for a Cost Flow Assumption

If a firm has more goods available for sale than it uses or sells, and if it finds specific identification not feasible or desirable, it must make some assumptions about the flow of costs. The accountant computes the acquisition cost applicable to the units sold and to the units remaining in the inventory using one of the following cost flow assumptions:

1. *First-in, first out (FIFO)* cost flow assumptions assigns the costs of the earliest units acquired to the withdrawals and assigns the cost of the most recent acquisitions to the ending inventory. This cost flow assumes that the firm uses the oldest materials and goods first.

    For example: A DVD player manufacturer has three identical items in stock as below:

Item	Date of Purchase	Cost
Item 1	1-Jan-05	$100
Item 2	1-Feb-05	$120
Item 3	1-Oct-05	$140

    The selling price of the final product is $200. What is the COGS, ending inventory, sales and gross margin for this company if it sells only one player in the year? Assume FIFO.

    Sales = $200

    COGS = $100 (since item 1 was purchased the earliest)

    Ending Inventory = $120+$140 = $260

    Gross Margin = Sales – COGS = $100

2. *Last-in, first out (LIFO)* cost flow assumptions assigns the costs of the latest units acquired to the withdrawals and assigns the cost of oldest acquisitions to the ending inventory. Some analysts believe that since LIFO matches current costs to current revenues; it is a better measure for income.

    Using the example above, for LIFO:

    Sales = $200

    COGS = $140 (since item 3 was purchased the latest)

    Ending Inventory = $100+$120 = $220

    Gross Margin = Sales – COGS = $60

3. *Weighted Average* cost flow assumption calculates the average of the cost of all goods available for sale. The weighted average cost applies to the units sold during the period and to units on hand at the end of the period.

Using the example above, for weighted average:

Sales = $200

COGS = $120 ((100+120+140)/3 =120)

Ending Inventory = $240 ($120*2 = $240)

Gross Margin = Sales – COGS = $80

Of the three cost flow assumptions, FIFO results in balance sheet figures that are the closes to the current cost because the latest purchases dominate the ending inventory amounts. The COGS expense tends to be out of date and when purchase prices rise, FIFO usually leads to reporting of a higher net income and when prices fall, it results in a lower net income.

LIFO ending inventory contains costs of items acquired long time back and thus when purchase prices rise, LIFO usually leads to reporting of a lower net income and when prices fall, it results in a higher net income. LIFO's COGS figure closely represents current costs.

Weighted average cost flow assumption falls in between FIFO and LIFO but it resembles FIFO more than LIFO in its impact on the financial statements.

Marketing

When it comes to marketing there are four basic elements which businesses can manipulate to best reach their target market. The four elements are product, price, place, and promotion. They are referred to as the marketing mix or the four P's. Product describes the physical good or service which the business provides. Examples of product decisions include name, packaging and warranty. Price describes the amount that the product is sold for. Examples of price decisions include discounting options, seasonal pricing and price strategy. Place is also referred to as distribution and describes where the product is sold and how it gets there. Examples of place decisions include inventory management and how the product will be distributed (by truck, ship or plane). Promotion describes how the product is advertised. Examples of promotion decisions include what the advertisements will say or look like, who the product is targeted at and other factors.

While some companies specialize in a specific product, often companies will sell a variety of products. For example, a company that sells shampoo will most likely also sell conditioner, hair spray and a variety of other hair care products. Similarly, a company which sells roller blades may also sell skateboards, bikes and other recreational equipment. The various products which a company sells is referred to as product mix. Often product mix is measured as the number of different products which a company produces, but it can also include elements such as the number or products lines, the number of variations on products or other factors.

Determining the right price for a product relies on an understanding of the economic relationship between supply and demand. When graphed, the amount which a company is willing to supply will slope upward because the higher the price the more the company will want to sell, whereas when the price is lower fewer companies are willing to supply products. On the other hand, when graphed the amount that people demand will slope downward. This is because at higher prices people are willing to buy less of a product than they are at lower prices.

Because the lines slope in different directions, at some point they will intersect. This intersection between supply and demand is referred to as equilibrium price. Although equilibrium price is the right price for the market, it doesn't necessarily mean that it is the preferred price. Companies would still clearly prefer to charge more if they could, and consumers would prefer to pay less if they could, but at the equilibrium price the amount that consumers are willing to buy happens to coincide with the amount companies are willing to provide, placing the market in equilibrium.

Opportunity cost is defined as the value of the best alternative not chosen. For example, if a company sells a car to someone for 20 thousand dollars, and could have sold it to a different person for 25 thousand dollars, the opportunity cost is 25 thousand dollars, and it could be interpreted that the company had really lost five thousand dollars. On the other hand, if by selling the car to another person the company could only have made 18 thousand dollars, then the company made a two thousand dollar profit by selling it to the first customer (after factoring in opportunity cost).

E-Commerce

The buying and selling of goods and services over the internet is referred to as e-commerce. There are four general formats through which e-commerce occurs: Business to Business (B2B), Business to Consumer (B2C), Consumer to Business (C2B) and Consumer to Consumer (C2C). The first form of e-commerce, B2B, includes situations in which businesses interact over the internet. If a grocery store, which is a business, finds and pays for boxes of cereal from a manufacturer, which is also a business, over the internet then it would be an example of B2B e-commerce. The second form B2C is the one that most people would think of. This is when companies sell products over the internet.

For example, many large supermarket chains also offer a full array of products which can be purchased online and delivered to customer's homes. Some companies even exist exclusively online. The third form of e-commerce, C2B, occurs when consumers post their payment offers or budgets for goods or services online, and businesses decide whether they are willing to accept at that price. In this way consumers can make offers to multiple companies at once without having to negotiate with them individually. The final form of e-commerce, C2C, describes sites which allow for direct negotiation between consumers. For example, online auction sites which allow individuals to post products they wish to sell, and search for products they wish to buy.

 # *International Business*

Importing and exporting are how countries trade goods and services with each other. An export is produced in one country and sold to another. Exports are a small percent of GDP for the U.S. unlike for countries such as Germany and the United Kingdom. Imports are currently how we spend 20% of our money – and it is steadily increasing.

Trade barriers are anything that makes it difficult (or creates ad barrier) to trade. One natural barrier to trade is distance. This increases the cost to transport a product. Another barrier is language. If you cannot communicate with your buyer, then you cannot initiate or complete a transaction. A protectionist is someone who proclaims "buy American." Their primary aim is to keep jobs, companies and industries inside the country. Currently, there is a lot of coverage in the news about jobs being outsourced to India.

A tariff is a duty or a tax that a government puts on products that are imported or exported from a country. Sometimes a country enacts an embargo. An embargo is a prohibition or suspension of a certain type of item, or anything from a certain country or region. For example, the U.S. has an embargo against ivory and some types of firearms. Each country chooses their own items (if any) on which to place an embargo.

While it is considered a legal form of trade restrictions and is not an act of war (that would be a blockade), an embargo is a strong diplomatic policy and is often used to send a message. Embargoes do not necessarily have to be all inclusive, but can be limited to specific products. For example, an embargo on flour would mean that a company could not import or export any flour. On the other hand, an embargo on trade with a certain country would mean that all products could still be exported or imported, just not to and from that specific country.

GATT is the General Agreement of Tariffs and Trade is a treaty designed to reduce trade barriers. NAFTA is the North American Free Trade Agreement which helps reduce trade barriers between the United States, Canada and Mexico. The primary purpose of NAFTA is to lower trading barriers and dealing with trade disputes. Basically, NAFTA created a free trade zone between the three countries. NAFTA is governed by three Secretariats (one from each country), and creates a method through which trade disputes between the three countries can be resolved.

The World Bank is a part of the United Nations that provides loans to countries for development projects. IMF is the International Monetary Fund, an agency that seeks to establish a way for countries to finance and pay off loans. IMF is affiliated with the World Bank.

A bill of lading is a document of title which is a contract between the shipper and the carrier (think you and Fedex). It also serves as a receipt for the products that the shipper has placed on the carrier.

When a company exports more than it imports it is considered a favorable balance of trade. This is referred to as a **trade surplus** (because the country is bringing in more money from abroad than it is spending). In this case, net exports would be positive. On the other hand, if a country imports more than it exports, the result is an unfavorable balance of trade referred to as a trade deficit. In the case of a trade deficit, the value of net exports is negative.

The value of the products a nation exports minus the value of the products they import is referred to as the balance of trade or net exports. The balance of trade is always measured over a specific period of time. For example, the United States generally measures its net exports over the period of a year. If a country were to import 20 billion dollars of goods and services in a year, and exported 30 billion dollars of goods and services in a year, then **net exports** would be 10 million dollars.

 # *Human Resource Management*

HAWTHORNE EFFECT

In 1927 a series of studies began at Western Electric Company in Hawthorne, Illinois. The first study was testing the assumption that the worker output would increase if the level of light in the plant was turned up. To test the theory, they took several female workers into a separate room in the factory and tested their output against a variety of lighting. Surprisingly, output increased regardless of the light level, until it was too dark to see and then it remained constant. Why? By taking the workers into another room at the plant, they had done something inadvertently, they had made the workers feel special. Experts coin this example to be the Hawthorne effect, which is where the interest in the people's problems effect the outcome, not the changes themselves.

THEORY X & Y

Theory X is a management approach where you believe that people dislike work and responsibility and are only motivated by money and other financial incentives. It also assumes that these people must be micro managed and supervised.

Theory Y is the assumption that all people enjoy work, and will control their own performance if you give them the chance. These people will want to do a good job and work better with a hands off approach.

PERSONNEL ADMINISTRATION

All resources in an organization need management, i.e., they are subjected to the processes of management viz., planning, organizing, directing and controlling. Building and machinery are physical resources. Stocks, bank balances are financial resources. People are human resources. While no other resource – capital, land, machines can talk back, only human resources can think and talk back and this makes management of this resource that much more difficult.

Personnel Administration is that branch of general management which: (a) looks into manpower resources of an organization (b) has a managerial function of planning, organizing, directing and controlling and an operative function of recruiting, developing, compensating, integrating human resources together with keeping records on manpower (c) aims at harmonious labor (d) aims to achieve organizational goals by integrating human resources.

The form "industrial relations" is a broader concept, which seeks to bring in harmonious relationship between labor, managements and the government of an industry.

Managing diversity is when you create a work environment where women, minorities and people with disabilities can perform and succeed on the job.

The term "labor management" normally defines the managing of manual workers of an organization. Working conditions and worker discipline together with the general recruitment, selection, compensation, etc., are dealt with by labor management.

The scope of "personnel management" is truly wider. It deals with the recruitment, selection, placement, training, compensation, working condition, etc., pertaining to all categories of personnel in an organization. Personnel administration also deals with generation of mutual trust, total co-operation and cohesive work force culture and maintaining cordial relations with trade unions.

Affirmative action is a detailed plan that a company makes to recruit women and minorities into positions and promotions. The glass ceiling is a term used to describe the attitudes and unwritten policies that have blocked women or any person from moving up the corporate ladder.

PERFORMANCE APPRAISALS

An organization's current human resources need timely evaluation of their capabilities in order to be ready for any future needs. There are two sources where managers look to appraise capabilities of human resources: (1) Personnel records (which are built on the applications submitted), and (2) Personnel Appraisal ratings. (1) Personnel records give all the data in the application together with high school, college and other educational institutional records, selection test scores, salary/wage started and changes made during the service, promotional opportunities availed, transfer effected, training courses attended, disciplinary actions, if any, recorded and personnel appraisal ratings. (2) Personnel Appraisal: The main purpose of any personnel appraisal plan is to help the employee to know his strengths and weaknesses, opportunities and threats (SWOT) and in order to build him for meeting ever increasing job challenges. Constructive criticism and helpful dialogue are excellent guidance for the employee to gain perspective and mental maturity to perform his allotted tasks skillfully and rise in the organization ladder. Companies rate many items pertaining to an individual and we give below an excerpt which will give a good idea of this concept.

Item Rated	Number of Times Found in 50 Merit-Rating Forms*
Group 1: The Old Standbys	
Quantity of work	44
Quality of work	31
Group 2: Job Knowledge and Performance	
Knowledge of job	25
Attendance	14
Punctuality	12
Safety habits	7

Good housekeeping	3
Group 3: Characteristics of the Individual	
Cooperativeness	36
Dependability	35
Initiative	27
Intelligence	17
Accuracy	14
Industry	14
Adaptability	14
Attitude	13
Personality	13
Judgment	12
Application	10
Leadership	6
Conduct	6
Resourcefulness	6
Health	5
Neatness	5
Appearance	4
Enthusiasm	4
Potential	4

*Integrity, loyalty, speech, tact and thoroughness were rated by three or fewer companies.
Source: "Marks of the Good Worker," National Industrial Conference Board Management Record, Vol. 18, No. 5 (May 1956), 168-70

Most companies have their own appraisal methods but the data normally sought to rate belongs to any one of the elements given above.

Good companies normally rate the person on the basis of his job-performance, attitude and behavior and then call the individual for personal counseling.

There are many methods of job evaluation and let us discuss some of them:

(1) <u>Ranking system</u>: In this jobs are ranked on the basis of responsibilities and duties and their importance to overall company objectives. Salary/wages are determined accordingly.

(2) <u>Classification method</u>: They define grades for requirements that are found common to various tasks on the basis of comparison between requirements regarding each task; they are classified with relevant grades.

(3) <u>Points system</u>: Requirements appropriate to each job are analyzed and quantified. Job requirements are subdivided into smaller degrees and each degree is assigned points. The total points a job gets determines its relative position vis-à-vis the job structure.

(4) <u>Factor Comparison</u>: For a few predetermined key jobs, points are allotted and wage rates for such key jobs are fixed. This will serve as a guiding factor for grading other jobs. Let us see three jobs of an organization now:

Job Requirements	Maximum Points	Maintenance Person	Machine Operator	Store Clerk
Experience	20.00	10.00	15.00	5.00
Job Knowledge and Job Skill	40.00	35.00	20.00	10.00
Negligence	20.00	15.00	10.00	5.00
Working Conditions	20.00	5.00	5.00	5.00
	100.00	65.00	50.00	25.00

The above organization fixes a basic pay of say $200 for all categories per month. In addition, the organization decides to pay $2 per point as per the above evaluation in which case the 3 job-men will receive:

	Maintenance Person $	Machine Operator $	Store Clerk $
Basic	200	200	200
Points Payment	130 (65*2)	100 (50*2)	50 (25*2)
	330.00	300.00	250.00

Collective Bargaining and Unions

Unions are formal associations of employees formed with a view to represent those employees in any dialogue to bargain collectively with the management. Their negotiations with the management include improved working conditions, better wage structures, less hours of work, more rest periods, etc., and generally work towards establishing good labor policies. In the USA 'organized' labor is a term normally used to distinguish members of unions from employees who do not have a formal union to support them. There are blue-collar as well as white-collar worker unions in the USA.

Unions use a process of discussion or negotiation between management and the union that represents the workers. Each side comes to the table with their own agenda and through time and compromise, reaches an agreement. This is a simplified version as most contracts take several rounds of negotiations regarding wages, etc. Once a formal agreement is reached both parties sign a typed contract. In these sessions, an arbitrator may be used. The arbitrator takes on the role of a judge and can determine what is "fair." An arbitrator also generally has the last word and has the power to complete the settlement. A mediator is a neutral third party that helps two parties reach an agreement. They do not have any power to "force" the sides to agree but help to keep negotiations on track. If the union decides to not negotiate anymore they call a "strike" where the workers do not come to work until the problem is resolved.

In reality, unions are mostly a thing of the past. Although they exist in some "trade" capacities still today, they actually hinder the American worker by not giving them the power to negotiate for themselves. If you manage union employees and you need to talk to them about their performance, you do not speak to them. Instead, you speak to the union and they speak to them for you. It adds an additional layer to the communication process, making it harder for businesses to manage their employees.

Also, unions involve dues which the member must pay. Unions also contribute to political groups and candidates whose views may or may not be the views of the member. The member does not have control over where his dues go or to whom they go.

Union groups are called "shops" instead of being called a company. A union shop can hire nonunion workers but they must pay dues and join the union within a set period of time. Some union shops are "closed shops"; they only hire union members. Although this is against the law, it still happens today. An agency shop includes member and nonmembers of the union but all are require to pay dues. Open shop is when they have both members and nonmembers work together, but only the union members pay dues.

The AFL-CIO or American Federation of Labor and Congress of Industrial Organizations is the large political body for unions. By voluntarily belonging to this organization, the members are receiving the benefits of their lobbying power in politics.

Union Member Rights

Bill of Rights - Union members have:
- Equal rights to participate in union activities
- Freedom of speech and assembly
- A voice in setting rates of dues, fees, and assessments
- Protection of the right to sue
- Safeguards against improper discipline

Copies of Collective Bargaining Agreements - Union members and nonunion employees have the right to receive or inspect copies of collective bargaining agreements.

Reports - Unions are required to file an initial information report, copies of constitutions and bylaws, and an annual financial report with OLMS. Unions must make the reports available to members and permit members to examine supporting records for just cause.

Officer Elections - Union members have the right to:
- Nominate candidates for office
- Run for office
- Cast a secret ballot
- Protest the conduct of an election

Officer Removal - Local union members have the right to an adequate procedure for the removal of an elected officer guilty of serious misconduct.

Trusteeships - Unions may only be placed in trusteeship by a parent body for the reasons specified in the LMRDA.

Prohibition Against Certain Discipline - A union or any of its officials may not fine, expel, or otherwise discipline a member for exercising any LMRDA right.

Prohibition Against Violence - No one may use or threaten to use force or violence to interfere with a union member in the exercise of LMRDA rights.

Union Officer Responsibilities

Financial Safeguards - Union officers have a duty to manage the funds and property of the union solely for the benefit of the union and its members in accordance with the union's constitution and bylaws. Union officers or employees who embezzle or steal union funds or other assets commit a Federal crime punishable by a fine and/or imprisonment.

Bonding - Union officers or employees who handle union funds or property must be bonded to provide protection against losses if their union has property and annual financial receipts which exceed $5,000.

Officer Reports - Union officers and employees must file reports concerning any loans and benefits received from, or certain financial interests in, employers whose employees their unions represent and businesses that deal with their unions.

Officer Elections - Unions must:

- Hold elections of officers of local unions by secret ballot at least every three years
- Conduct regular elections in accordance with their constitution and bylaws and preserve all records for one year
- Mail a notice of election to every member at least 15 days prior to the election
- Comply with a candidate's request to distribute campaign material
- Not use union funds or resources to promote any candidate (nor may employer funds or resources be used)
- Permit candidates to have election observers
- Allow candidates to inspect the union's membership list once within 30 days prior to the election

Restrictions on Holding Office - A person convicted of certain crimes may not serve as a union officer, employee, or other representative of a union for up to 13 years.

Loans - A union may not have outstanding loans to any one officer or employee that in total exceed $2,000 at any time.

Fines - A union may not pay the fine of any officer or employee convicted of any willful violation of the LMRDA.

 # Taft Hartley Act

In 1947, Congress passed the Taft Hartley Act which outlawed for unions the closed shop, jurisdictional strikes, and secondary boycotts. It set up machinery for decertifying unions and allowed the states to pass more stringent legislation against unions such as right to work laws. Employers and unions were forbidden to contribute funds out of their treasuries to candidates for federal office, supervision was denied union protection, and the unions seeking the services of the National Labor Relations Board had to file their constitutions, by laws, and financial statements with the U.S. Department of Labor. Their officers also had to sign a non communist affidavit.

NLRA and NLRB

The National Labor Relations Board is an independent federal agency created by Congress in 1935 to administer the National Labor Relations Act (NLRA), the primary law governing relations between unions and employers in the private sector. The statute guarantees the right of employees to organize and to bargain collectively with their employers or to refrain from all such activity. Generally applying to all employers involved in interstate commerce – other than airlines, railroads, agriculture, and government – the Act implements the national labor policy of assuring free choice and encouraging collective bargaining as a means of maintaining industrial peace. Through the years, Congress has amended the Act and the Board and courts have developed a body of law drawn from the statute.

What Does the NLRB Do?

In its statutory assignment, the NLRB has two principal functions: (1) to determine, through [secret-ballot elections,] the free democratic choice by employees whether they wish to be represented by a union in dealing with their employers and if so, by which union; and (2) to prevent and remedy unlawful acts, called [unfair labor practices,] by either employers or unions. The agency does not act on its own motion in either function. It processes only those charges of unfair labor practices and petitions for employee elections that are filed with the NLRB in one of its 51 Regional, Subregional, or Resident Offices.

What Is the NLRB's Structure?

The agency has two major, separate components.

The Board itself has five Members and primarily acts as a quasi-judicial body in deciding cases on the basis of formal records in administrative proceedings. Board Members are appointed by the President to 5-year terms, with Senate consent, the term of one Member expiring each year. The current Members are Robert J. Battista (Chairman), Wilma B. Liebman, Peter C. Schaumber, Peter N. Kirsanow, and Dennis P. Walsh.

The General Counsel, appointed by the President to a 4-year term with Senate consent, is independent from the Board and is responsible for the investigation and prosecution of unfair labor practice cases and for the general supervision of the NLRB field offices in the processing of cases. The current General Counsel is Ronald Meisburg. Each Regional Office is headed by a Regional Director who is responsible for making the initial determination in cases arising within the geographical area served by the region.

How Are Unfair Labor Practice Cases Processed?

When an unfair labor practice (ULP) charge is filed, the appropriate field office conducts an investigation to determine whether there is reasonable cause to believe the Act has been violated. If the Regional Director determines that the charge lacks merit, it will be dismissed unless the charging party decides to withdraw the charge. A dismissal may be appealed to the General Counsel's office in Washington, D.C.

If the Regional Director finds reasonable cause to believe a violation of the law has been committed, the region seeks a voluntary settlement to remedy the alleged violations. If these settlement efforts fail, a formal complaint is issued and the case goes to hearing before an NLRB Administrative Law Judge. The judge issues a written decision that may be appealed to the five- Member Board in Washington for a final agency determination. The Board's decision is subject to review in a U.S. Court of Appeals. Depending upon the nature of the case, the General Counsel's goal is to complete investigations and, where further proceedings are warranted, issue complaints if settlement is not reached within 7 to 15 weeks from the filing of the charge. Of the total ULP charges filed each year [about 25,000], approximately one-third are found to have merit of which over 90% are settled.

 # *Training and Development*

The process of hiring new employees extends beyond simply choosing a new employee. For example, most jobs will require some amount of training. Two types of training are on the job training and vestibule training. On the job training is training which a person is expected to pick up as they go, or learn through doing the work. It can also include showing them how the specific machines or programs operate, for example. The point is though that they are trained with the actual equipment that they will be using. Vestibule training, on the other hand, simulates the environment in which employees will be working. For example, astronauts have to train for their missions into space, but must receive vestibule training. New employees will also often receive orientations during which they fill out necessary paperwork and are given a tour of their working environment. They will also be introduced to the people that they are working with and other necessary introduction activities.

Training can be considered as a program built primarily to assist employee development. There are various kinds of training in vogue: (1) Apprenticeship (2) Refresher courses (3) Promotional training (4) On the job training (5) Off the job training, etc. The specific purposes behind training are:

(1) Knowledge and skill enhancement
(2) Makes it possible to introduce new methods. Encourages people to introduce new methods thereby making it possible for the personnel to work more effectively and efficiently.

(3) Knowledge on safety. It provides the much needed knowledge on how to operate machines without any risk.

(4) Latest techniques: Training impacts latest techniques available and makes the operator much more skillful and technique-oriented.

(5) Morale boosting: Promotes self-confidence of personnel as they are trained in skills, knowledge, aptitude and attitude necessary to do their job most efficiently.

(6) Self-actualization: It paves the way for employees to realize their full potential.

Many corporate business houses have substantial training budgets to augment and fine tune their managerial skills. On the job training for managers include:

(1) Planned progression

(2) Temporary promotion

(3) Job rotation

(4) The committee method

(5) Coaching

Training needs are to be analyzed before arriving at the training program. How is need analyzed? A hypothetical case study:

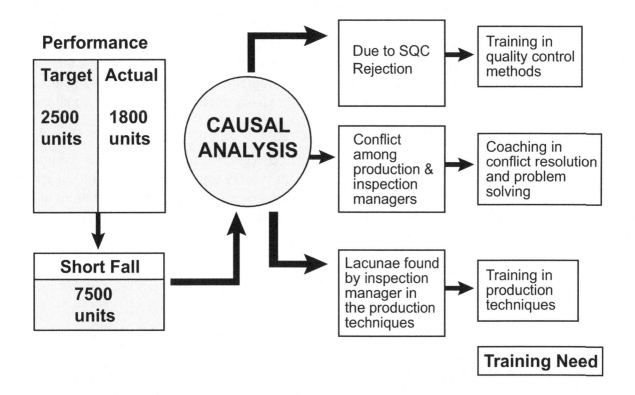

TRAINING NEED ANALYSIS

Training may consist of:

1) Coaching

2) Conference

3) Group dynamics

4) Idea tracking

5) Managerial games

6) Multimedia presentations

7) Role playing

8) Programmed learning

9) T Group

10) Workshop, and

11) Special tuition

ORGANIZATIONAL DEVELOPMENT – OD

Organizational development – simply OD – is a methodical, integrated and a well thought out and well planned approach that seeks to improve organizational effectiveness. The design generally reveals solutions to problems that threaten or are already impeding operating efficiency of the organization at all levels. It may be ineffective communication, or excessive centralization, or extreme decentralization, and/or even willful apathy amounting to non-cooperation. The solutions to problems are found in team building programs, job enrichment programs, programs meant for organizational behavior modification, or simple MBO (Management by Objective), which we have already seen.

The normal organizational development process first aims to recognize the problems correctly, then diagnoses the problems, then seeks data and information feedback, then begins designing and developing a change strategy with proper interventions and then establishes yardsticks for effective evaluation of the change.

COBRA

COBRA stands for The Comprehensive Omnibus Budget Reconciliation Act. It requires employers to allow employees to retain medical insurance after they quit or are terminated, for up to 18 months. It gives workers and their families who lose their health benefits the right to choose to continue group health benefits provided by their group health plan for limited periods of time under certain circumstances such as voluntary or involuntary job loss, reduction in the hours worked, transition between jobs, death, divorce, and other life events. Qualified individuals may be required to pay the entire premium for coverage up to 102 percent of the cost to the plan.

COBRA generally requires that group health plans sponsored by employers with 20 or more employees in the prior year offer employees and their families the opportunity for a temporary extension of health coverage (called continuation coverage) in certain instances where coverage under the plan would otherwise end.

COBRA outlines how employees and family members may elect continuation coverage. It also requires employers and plans to provide notice.

OSHA

OSHA stands for the Occupational Safety & Health Administration. OSHA's mission is to assure the safety and health of America's workers by setting and enforcing standards; providing training, outreach, and education; establishing partnerships; and encouraging continual improvement in workplace safety and health.

Nearly every working man and woman in the nation comes under OSHA's jurisdiction (with some exceptions such as miners, transportation workers, many public employees, and the self-employed). Other users and recipients of OSHA services include: occupational safety and health professionals, the academic community, lawyers, journalists, and personnel of other government entities.

The United States Department of Labor is in charge of making sure companies are in compliance with federal employment laws.

OSHA has four levels of priorities:

1. Inspect for immediately dangerous circumstances/locations
2. Research catastrophes, accidents or deaths involving five people or more
3. Investigate employee concerns about an unsafe working environment
4. Inspections for companies and industries with hazardous or high injury to health

Companies that have repeat, serious or willful violations can be charged fines up to $70,000.

 **EEO**

EEO stands for Equal Employment Opportunity. This is a commission that investigates and prosecutes those business and individuals who discriminate against protected classes, such as discrimination involving:

- Age
- Disability
- Equal Pay
- National Origin
- Pregnancy
- Race
- Religion
- Retaliation
- Sex
- Sexual Harassment

Equal Pay Act of 1963

No employer having employees subject to any provisions of this section shall discriminate, within any establishment in which such employees are employed, between employees on the basis of sex by paying wages to employees in such establishment at a rate less than the rate at which he pays wages to employees of the opposite sex in such establishment for equal work on jobs the performance of which requires equal skill, effort, and responsibility, and which are performed under similar working conditions, except where such payment is made pursuant to:

(i) a seniority system
(ii) a merit system
(iii) a system which measures earnings by quantity or quality of production;
(iv) a differential based on any other factor other than sex, provided that an employer who is paying a wage rate differential in violation of this subsection shall not, in order to comply with the provisions of this subsection, reduce the wage rate of any employee.

Another word for equal pay is comparable worth generally used in this same context. Comparable worth is the idea that men and women should be paid equal wages for doing comparable work. Some companies use a comparable worth point system (similar to a job grade) to equal out employee pay.

 *ERISA*

The Employee Retirement Income Security Act of 1974 (ERISA) is a federal law that sets minimum standards for most voluntarily established pension and health plans in private industry to provide protection for individuals in these plans.

ERISA requires plans to provide participants with plan information including important information about plan features and funding; provides fiduciary responsibilities for those who manage and control plan assets; requires plans to establish a grievance and appeals process for participants to get benefits from their plans; and gives participants the right to sue for benefits and breaches of fiduciary duty.

There have been a number of amendments to ERISA, expanding the protections available to health benefit plan participants and beneficiaries. One important amendment, the Consolidated Omnibus Budget Reconciliation Act (COBRA), provides some workers and their families with the right to continue their health coverage for a limited time after certain events, such as the loss of a job. Another amendment to ERISA is the

Health Insurance Portability and Accountability Act (HIPAA), which provides important new protections for working Americans and their families who have preexisting medical conditions or might otherwise suffer discrimination in health coverage based on factors that relate to an individual's health. Other important amendments include the Newborns' and Mothers' Health Protection Act, the Mental Health Parity Act, and the Women's Health and Cancer Rights Act.

In general, ERISA does not cover group health plans established or maintained by governmental entities, churches for their employees, or plans which are maintained solely to comply with applicable workers compensation, unemployment, or disability laws. ERISA also does not cover plans maintained outside the United States primarily for the benefit of nonresident aliens or unfunded excess benefit plans.

 # ADA

Title I of the Americans with Disabilities Act (ADA) prohibits employers of 15 or more workers, employment agencies, and labor organizations of 15 or more workers from discriminating against qualified individuals with disabilities.

Title II of the Americans with Disabilities Act (ADA) prohibits state and local governments from discriminating against qualified individuals with disabilities in programs, activities, and services.

The Vietnam Era Veterans' Readjustment Assistance Act (VEVRAA) prohibits discrimination against and requires affirmative action for qualified special disabled veterans, as well as other categories of veterans. This law is enforced by the OFCCP.

Section 188 of the Workforce Investment Act of 1998 (WIA) prohibits discrimination against qualified individuals with disabilities who are applicants, employees, and participants in WIA Title I-financially assisted programs and activities, and programs that are part of the One-Stop system. Section 188 also prohibits discrimination on the grounds of age, race, color, religion, sex, national origin, political affiliation or belief, and for beneficiaries only, citizenship or participation in a WIA Title I-financially assisted program or activity. This law is enforced by the Civil Rights Center.

UCC

The Uniform Commercial Code was first published in 1952. It's main purpose is to regulate inter-state trade through a list of rules and regulations. UCC is not a federal law, but pieces of the code have been adopted by each state to help regulate business.

FMLA

The Family and Medical Leave Act (FMLA) provides certain employees with up to 12 weeks of unpaid, job-protected leave per year. It also requires that their group health benefits be maintained during the leave.

FMLA is designed to help employees balance their work and family responsibilities by allowing them to take reasonable unpaid leave for certain family and medical reasons. It also seeks to accommodate the legitimate interests of employers and promote equal employment opportunity for men and women.

FMLA applies to all public agencies, all public and private elementary and secondary schools, and companies with 50 or more employees. These employers must provide an eligible employee with up to 12 weeks of unpaid leave each year for any of the following reasons:

- for the birth and care of the newborn child of an employee;
- for placement with the employee of a child for adoption or foster care;
- to care for an immediate family member (spouse, child, or parent) with a serious health condition; or
- to take medical leave when the employee is unable to work because of a serious health condition.

Employees are eligible for leave if they have worked for their employer at least 12 months, at least 1,250 hours over the past 12 months, and work at a location where the company employs 50 or more employees within 75 miles. Whether an employee has worked the minimum 1,250 hours of service is determined according to FLSA principles for determining compensable hours or work.

Time taken off work due to pregnancy complications can be counted against the 12 weeks of family and medical leave.

Special rules apply to employees of local education agencies. The Department of Labor administers FMLA; however, the Office of Personnel Management (OPM) administers FMLA for most federal employees.

Wage and Salary Administration

Compensation is whatever money employees are paid to perform a task or function. Employees can be paid by the hour, by the piece or be salaried. Compensation also includes anything they receive such as bonuses, paid time off, vacation, 401k, etc.

A common problem for employers is establishing fair wages across the board. This can be a major internal problem when a more tenured employee discovers they are earning less than a new hire. To establish pay rates in the corporate world, there are several steps to make this a more structured process. The more processes you have, the less likelihood of having legal problems in the future based on pay.

First, you may begin with a salary survey to determine what the going rate is for a specific job. We'll use the example of a secretary. To find out, you can contact employment agencies, look online and in the newspaper. We use these numbers as a benchmark. The process is then repeated for other major jobs in the organization.

Each job is then evaluated by compensable factors including:

- Responsibility
- Experience
- Skills
- Working conditions

These are used to show how much more or less is required from job to job. The easiest way to rank jobs is to use categories, classes and grades. Each pay grade is a certain number. For example, grade 6 will equate to $24,000 per year. Grade 22 will equate to $42,000 per year. You can then assign particular grades to certain job functions.

Rate ranges give you a way to pay employees in the same job title different amounts. All may be account managers but some may have more experience. Pay rates can be created based on the information from pay grades. Plot the salaries from each pay grade and using an arc line, plot your data. These can be your target wages.

However, keep in mind that this is a relatively old process for determining pay rates and is not used as much today as in the past. The most popular form of compensation is based on performance for the company.

Wages

Workweek - A workweek is a period of 168 hours during 7 consecutive 24-hour periods. It may begin on any day of the week and at any hour of the day established by the employer. Generally, for purposes of minimum wage and overtime payment, each workweek stands alone; there can be no averaging of 2 or more workweeks. Employee coverage, compliance with wage payment requirements, and the application of most exemptions are determined on a workweek basis.

Hours Worked - Covered employees must be paid for all hours worked in a workweek. In general, "hours worked" includes all time an employee must be on duty, or on the employer's premises or at any other prescribed place of work. Also included is any additional time the employee is allowed (i.e., suffered or permitted) to work.

Overtime must be paid at a rate of at least one and one-half times the employee's regular rate of pay for each hour worked in a workweek in excess of the maximum allowable in a given type of employment. Generally, the regular rate includes all payments made by the employer to or on behalf of the employee (except for certain statutory exclusions). The following examples are based on a maximum 40-hour workweek.

Hourly rate (regular pay rate for an employee paid by the hour) - If more than 40 hours are worked, at least one and one-half times the regular rate for each hour over 40 is due.

Example: An employee paid $8.00 an hour works 44 hours in a workweek. The employee is entitled to at least one and one-half times $8.00, or $12.00, for each hour over 40. Pay for the week would be $320 for the first 40 hours, plus $48.00 for the four hours of overtime - a total of $368.00.

Piece rate - The regular rate of pay for an employee paid on a piecework basis is obtained by dividing the total weekly earnings by the total number of hours worked in that week. The employee is entitled to an additional one-half times this regular rate for each hour over 40, plus the full piecework earnings.

Example: An employee paid on a piecework basis works 45 hours in a week and earns $315. The regular rate of pay for that week is $315 divided by 45, or $7.00 an hour. In addition to the straight-time pay, the employee is also entitled to $3.50 (half the regular rate) for each hour over 40 - an additional $17.50 for the 5 overtime hours - for a total of $332.50.

Another way to compensate pieceworkers for overtime, if agreed to before the work is performed, is to pay one and one-half times the piece rate for each piece produced during the overtime hours. The piece rate must be the one actually paid during non-overtime hours and must be enough to yield at least the minimum wage per hour.

Commission - This is when employees are paid rewards based on a percentage of their sales. When an employee is paid salary and commission it is called a combination plan.

Salary - The regular rate for an employee paid a salary for a regular or specified number of hours a week is obtained by dividing the salary by the number of hours for which the salary is intended to compensate.

If, under the employment agreement, a salary sufficient to meet the minimum wage requirement in every workweek is paid as straight time for whatever number of hours is worked in a workweek, the regular rate is obtained by dividing the salary by the number of hours worked each week. To illustrate, suppose an employee's hours of work vary each week and the agreement with the employer is that the employee will be paid $420 a week for whatever number of hours of work is required. Under this agreement, the regular rate will vary in overtime weeks. If the employee works 50 hours, the regular rate is $8.40 ($420 divided by 50 hours). In addition to the salary, half the regular rate, or $4.20, is due for each of the 10 overtime hours, for a total of $462 for the week. If the employee works 60 hours, the regular rate is $7.00 ($420 divided by 60 hours). In that case, an additional $3.50 is due for each of the 20 overtime hours for a total of $490 for the week.

In no case may the regular rate be less than the minimum wage required by FLSA.

If a salary is paid on other than a weekly basis, the weekly pay must be determined in order to compute the regular rate and overtime pay. If the salary is for a half month, it must be multiplied by 24 and the product divided by 52 weeks to get the weekly equivalent. A monthly salary should be multiplied by 12 and the product divided by 52.

 # *Piecework*

Under the Fair Labor Standards Act (FLSA), industrial homework (also called "piecework") means the production by any covered person in a home, apartment, or room in a residential establishment, of goods for an employer who permits or authorizes such production, regardless of the source (whether obtained from an employer or elsewhere) of the materials used by the home worker in producing these items.

The performance of certain types of industrial homework is prohibited under the FLSA unless the employer has obtained prior certification from the Department of Labor. Restrictions apply in the manufacture of knitted outerwear, gloves and mittens, buttons and buckles, handkerchiefs, embroideries, and jewelry, if there are no safety and health hazards. The manufacture of women's apparel (and jewelry under hazardous conditions) is generally prohibited. All individually covered homework is subject to the FLSA's minimum wage, overtime, and record keeping requirements. Employers must provide workers with handbooks to record time, expenses, and pay information.

 # Operational Aspects of Management

INFORMATION PROCESSING AND MANAGEMENT

The main managerial function is to get things done by making things happen and not piously hoping for desired results to materialize and wishing problems to evaporate. To get things done through others – the essence of managing – in an organizational backdrop requires precise informational flow for a manager. Without precise information from above and from below, a manager finds it difficult to take proper direction and provide proper action plans.

Today, thanks to the Information Technology Revolution, there is an abundant cascade of information, a veritable information system. Instead of hunting for info today we choose from among a bewildering variety of information on any subject.

A manager needs information in order to effectively focus on the functions such as planning, organizing, directing and controlling. The policies of management in the areas of inventories, customer service, scheduling, etc., are developed from information and data generated from production control functions. Likewise information on the competitors' activities, market standing, competitors' overall strategies, their offer of inducements, their planning to introduce new products, etc., are gleaned from the market by salesmen, by wholesalers, by distributors, by retailers and by friendly salesmen of competitors. Such information whether for production or for marketing is essential for managers to process, analyze and use effectively to succeed in accomplishing overall organizational objectives.

Information and data processing in an organization:

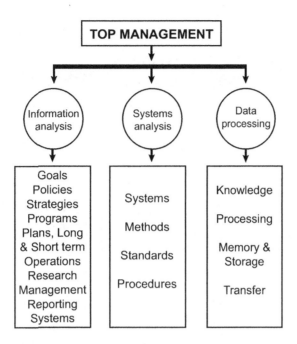

OPERATIONS PLANNING AND CONTROL

A simple illustration of Operations Management

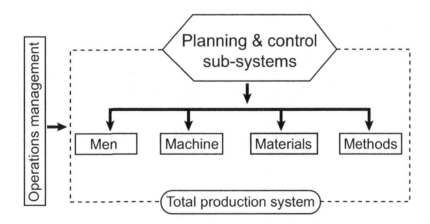

Operations Management can be defined as the planning, organizing, executing and controlling of an organization's total production system through optimal use of the factors that contribute to the planning and control subsystems, viz., Men, Machines, Materials and Methods, and in the process suggesting effective improvement for the total production system.

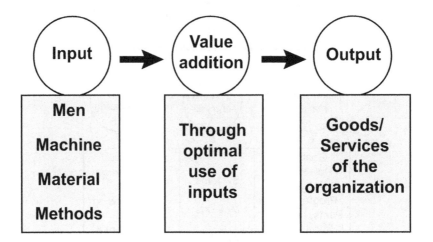

Any production system thinks in terms of excellent customer service, investment on inventory and effective utilization of resources resulting in minimal cost of plant operations. A good production control system always centers around:

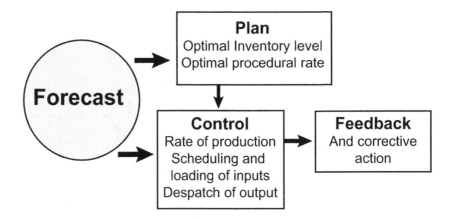

There are a few important steps in Production Planning Forecasting: (1) Preparation of essential information and data (2) Working on the forecast, and (3) Tracking the forecast.

In a factory "Lead time" means the time it takes to get an inventory item – from ordering to arrival and taking into stock. In planning production you have to take into account (a) set up time (b) production time (c) queue time (d) movement time, and (e) waiting time. A typical production plan:

PISTON – 4 STROKE (IN PIECES)

Date	Sales	Production	Inventory
Opening Balance	–	–	15,000
10/9/2000	7,000.00	8,000.00	16,000
11/9/2000	5,000.00	10,000.00	21,000
12/9/2000	10,000.00	7,000.00	18,000
13/9/2000	10,000.00	8,000.00	16,000
14/9/2000	9,000.00	9,000.00	16,000
15/9/2000	8,000.00	6,000.00	14,000
Closing Balance	–	–	14,000

Another new concept in inventory is called JIT or just in time inventory. This is the idea that you only get supplies, products and inventory right before they are needed. Walmart is a great example of using JIT inventory. Their extensive database monitors what is selling in what store and only sends exactly what each store needs, right before they run out. Walmart is also the biggest retailer in the U.S.

PRODUCTIVITY

Productivity is a very complex issue as it depends on a host of variables, some of which may not be easily predictable and therefore must be taken into account. The design of the job itself is a complex factor. Technology is another. Human and managerial facts lend more complexity. Add to these the external factors; you have an issue which is complex and sophisticated at the same time. In its rudimentary equation, productivity relates to the input-output ratio meant for a given time period. The constant factor of course is quality as there is no compromise on that score in any organization. If given expression, a productivity equation looks like the one given below:

$$Productivity = Output/Input$$

Suppose, a tailor, Mr. X, in a normal shift of 8 hours stitches 40 medium sized shirts. Mr. X's productivity 40/8 = 5 shirts per machine hour. The productivity here is measured in terms of units produced per machine hour worked. Increased effectiveness and total efficiency are the hallmarks of increased productivity.

TOTAL QUALITY MANAGEMENT (TQM)

Quality of a product determines its salability. Products enjoying exceptional quality standards demand a premium. There should be a conscious effort to maintain a high quality in not only the end product, but even the methods, systems, communication and thinking of top level to the floor level employee. A good quality program includes:

(1) Determination of standards of quality

(2) Institution of an effective continuous on the job checking program with responsibilities and accountability firmly fixed

(3) A recording system for comparing errors vs. standards

(4) A method which spells out corrective action, and

(5) To install a program of analysis and quality improvement whenever found needed.

Checking on the production line while the job is on is a good system. However, it may not be possible to check every piece produced. Here the statistical quality methods come to help. Normally checking is done on a random basis (Random Sampling Method). The most common program liked by organizations is the <u>acceptance sampling</u> method. A sample, normally 10 to 15% of a batch from a running production line, is checked. If they find that a high majority of the checked batch quantities consistently match the set standards for qualitative accuracy, the entire batch (the balance of 90 to 85% as the case may be) is accepted. This is acceptance sampling in essence.

For companies and organizations in the public and private sectors - there is a prestigious award that recognizes excellence. It is called the Malcolm Baldrige National Quality Award and is given by the President of the United States for performance excellence. up to 18 awards can be given annually.

ISO

The ISO 9000, like the ISO 14000, is a group of classification which companies can work to achieve classification in. The ISO 9000 classification is primarily concerned with ensuring that companies are maintaining the interests of their stakeholders. For example, some aspects of the standard are that companies have adequate planning when they begin a new product, that they ensure that bad products aren't taken to market and that the business regularly has product and quality evaluations.

The ISO itself doesn't certify companies, but rather many independent organizations have been set up which examine a company to determine whether it is worthy to achieve the classification. These organizations charge a fee, so not all companies choose to obtain ISO certification. Also, certifications have to be renewed periodically because they are not indefinite.

The ISO 14000 is an international standard for environmental management and awareness. It is set forth by the International Organization for Standardization which works to place companies across the world on similar standards. There are many different levels of ISO 14000 standards all of which are voluntary. For example the ISO 14001 and 14004 standards require that a company create an Environmental Management System (EMS). The standard doesn't set forth specific goals or limits, but rather simply requires that companies have an EMS and hold to it. The standards are a set of guidelines specifying how the business should go about creating and executing their EMS systems.

Although it is not an actual law, the ISO 14001 is a standard that companies can voluntarily follow in improving their environmental safety. ISO stands for International Standardization Organization. The organization has standardizations for all different areas, but the 14001 standard applies to environmental issues. ISO 14001 is a voluntary program of continual improvement. It is not a specific standard which companies must meet, but rather provides a framework which businesses can use to get started. Under ISO 14001 a company develops its own set of objectives and goals. The company then implements processes in an effort to meet these goals. The company should then consider how well the processes are helping them meet their goals and find ways to continue to improve.

Today there is ISO-9000 (which tells us that a well thought out system will produce predicted quality consistently, with consistency in the implementation of the system at every stage – not only in design or production but in policies and actions of all employees), TQM – Total Quality Management (which tells us to continuously meet agreed customer requirements at the lowest cost, by realizing the potential of employees). 6-Sigma Concept (which tells us that, when a product is rated as 6-Sigma, it means that the product exhibits no more than 3.4 non conformities per million opportunities (NPMO) at the part and process levels). All these concepts aim to give a zero-defect product.

The quality movement has acquired many gurus. Chief among them are: (1) Phillip B. Crosby – who always emphasized "zero-defect," (2) Dr. W. Edwards Deming – who is considered the forefather of the Japanese quality revolution and the thrust of his philosophy has always been planned reduction of variation, and (3) Dr. Joseph Juran – who always thought and taught that quality is achievable through people rather than technique.

WORK SCHEDULING

An effective and most efficient production control system always assigns a prominent role to work scheduling. There are input scheduling and output scheduling. In input scheduling input control is divided into: (1) Order Selection, i.e., the right orders for feeding into the machines. This is based on planned production rate or customs order, or material control system. (2) Scheduling – after considering the operations to be performed on each production order, they allot times and arrive at the completion date. (3) Loading – this involves the working out of hours required to perform each operation and then compares that factor with availability of work hours in each cost (work) center. The capacity planning vis-à-vis the machine, operations, operator, etc., tells you what would be your job flow rate. Let us see the normal scheduling steps:

Provide Data	Sequencing of operations	**Develop systems**	Scheduling procedures Shop calendar	**Choice of scheduling method**	Forward scheduling Backward scheduling

In scheduling one has to: (1) multiply order quality by time per each operation. (2) To the number arrived at 1, add time of transit, and (3) provide for unexpected delays converting it to hours and add to total of 1+2.

Forward Scheduling: Starts today and works out the schedule date for each operation in order to find out the completion date for the order.

Backward Scheduling: Starts with the date on which the completed order is needed in the stores department for shipping, then works out backwards to determine the relevant release date for the order.

Marketing Decision Variables: In any company's marketing program, it is the Marketing Decision Variables that are bound to play a very important role. The best classification of marketing decision variables was given by E. Jerome McCarthy – the "Four P's" – (1) Product (2) Place (3) Promotion and (4) Price.

Marketing Mix: It is the most important task of the Marketing Department to find out the optimum setting for its Marketing Decision Variables. This Optimum Setting is considered the Marketing Mix of the company.

Marketing Effort: Refers to a company's employment of inputs, such as men, material and money, into the company's overall marketing process in order to generate sales.

Marketing Allocation: It refers to a company's allocation of total marketing efforts to its various products, different customer segments, different salesmen and different sales divisions.

Marketing Strategy: It refers to a company's overall objectives, tactics, policies and guidelines that govern over a period of that company's marketing effort.

The strategy spells out the total allocation, the ideal mix required and the level of marketing efforts needed to achieve a predetermined target. Environmental changes and the level of competitive thrust determine the overall strategy.

Consumer Market and an Analysis of Buyer Behavior

Today all markets are complex and unique. To understand the essentials of markets, a marketing system needs a general framework, which tries to understand the market's composition, character, needs and wants. There are four questions that will give an insight into this system.

1. What did the market use to buy? This gives you an insight into the <u>objects</u> of purchase.
2. Why buy? This gives an insight into the <u>objectives</u> of such purchases.
3. Who is buying? This gives an insight into the <u>organization</u> for such purchases.
4. How does it buy? This gives an insight into the general <u>working of the organization</u> that effects purchasing.

<u>THE FOUR P'S OR THE COMPONENTS OF MARKETING DECISION VARIABLES</u>

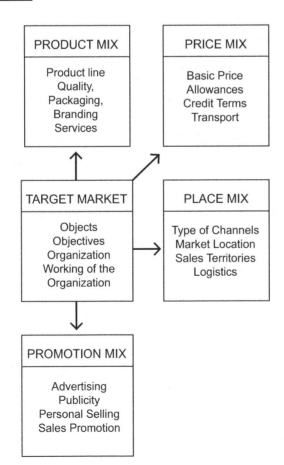

According to the specific characteristics of individual markets, the 4-P's of Marketing Decision variables are set. In a market where price is most sensitive, the organization tries to maintain the existing price levels even if a price increase from the organization's point of view is justified; it may offer more liberal credit terms or allow some allowances on the basis of more off-take, etc.

Consumer Markets: It is a market where product and services are purchased or hired solely for non-business (personal) consumption. The purchases are made by individuals or households. In the USA consumer markets are huge catering to more than 300 million individuals and families who consume products and services worth many trillions of US Dollars. Marketing people have recognized the existence of different groups and sub-groups within a given market and have developed strategies to cater to each group by developing products and services most suited to their varying needs. They segregate sub groups like: (1) Men, (2) Women, (3) Children, (4) Youth, and (5) Elderly – and offer differentiated products to suit the individual consumer of each such sub group. Having said that, it is better now for us to postulate a basis for the classification or grouping of a huge number of consumer products so we can get an insight into underlying marketing differences and implications on the Marketing Mix front.

DURABLE GOODS – NON-DURABLE GOODS AND SERVICES

Durable Goods: These tangible goods (actual goods), once bought, will satisfy you for many years (example: air conditioners, refrigerators, clothing, etc.).

Non-Durable Goods: These are also tangible goods, which once bought may be consumed in a very short period of time (example: toothpaste, soap, ham, biscuits, etc.).

Services: These are non-tangible activities, benefits and satisfactions that are offered by individuals with expertise (example: tailoring, hair dressing, cleaning, general repairing, etc.).

The general characteristics in relation to marketing of durable, non-durable and services are:

<u>Durable goods</u> – Needs more personal selling, more seller guarantees and to charge a higher margin.

Non-durable goods and services – To develop loyalty over time, marketed in a number of locations, charging a small margin. Any marketing strategy should be tailored to meet these general characteristics.

Another classification based on consumer's purchasing habits gives us three different groups of goods:

(1) Convenient Goods: Goods bought by consumers most often with relative speed without spending time on comparison (Example: Newspapers, soaps, detergents, tobacco products, etc.).

(2) Shopping Goods: Goods bought by consumers after spending time considering its utility, value, quality, suitability, style and of course, price (Example: Cars, home appliances, dress materials, furniture, etc.).

(3) Specialty Goods: Goods bought by consumers that have characteristics perceived to be unique and/or having good brand identification (Example: Branded goods, fancy goods, electronic goods, photographic equipment, etc.).

CONSUMER BEHAVIOR

What are the objectives or goals a consumer while effecting a purchase is looking for? To put it simply, he is looking for a perceived need satisfaction. Needs are unlimited.

Maslow's Hierarchy of Needs

Maslow's Hierarchy of Needs consists of the following stages from the top down:

- Self Actualization
- Esteem Needs
- Belonging and Love
- Safety
- Physical Needs

These stages begin at the physical needs. First you need to have food, water, and shelter before you can worry about other requirements. Once those needs are met you may start to think of other necessities, such as safety. You might buy a gun or move to a more prosperous and safe area. Once you are fed, clothed and safe you will want to meet needs of belonging and love through relationships. If you feel loved, you may begin to think about your self-esteem and how you feel as a person, what you are contributing. The final stage, self-actualization, you may never meet. Most people do not.

A Buyer's buying decisions are generally influenced by the Buyer's cultural, social, personal and psychological factors. We will presently see all those factors that influence Buyer behavior.

Factors Influencing Buyer Behavior

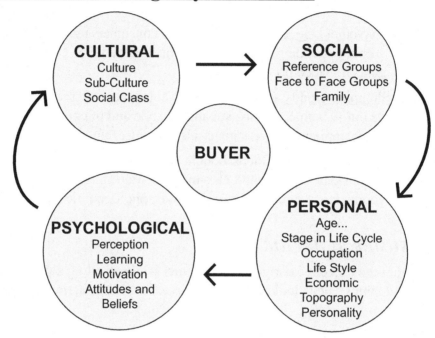

INTERNATIONAL BUSINESS

Gross National Product is a sum of a country's goods and services produced anywhere in the world. For example, a company in China can have manufacturing plants in the U.S. and in Mexico. The goods produced at those locations would still be included in the GNP.

Gross Domestic Product or GDP is the sum of all final goods and services produced in a country. This would include an Italian company that manufactures something in another country.

Four Asian countries are referred to as the Four Tigers. These countries include Taiwan, Honk Kong, Singapore and South Korea.

Patents are a way to legally protect your idea by preventing other companies from copying your invention. A patent expires after 17 years.

SPECIFIC CASE STUDIES

Joe Camel is the cartoon character created by R. J. Reynolds Tobacco Company to appeal and market to underage buyers. He is as much or more recognizable to children as Mickey Mouse.

Energizer battery has commercials and ad campaigns designed around a drum-banging pink bunny.

FINANCIAL MANAGEMENT

A CPA is an acronym for a Certified Public Accountant. A bull market is when stock prices on average are rising. Junk Bonds are bonds that are rated below Mood's and Standard and Poor's rating or AAA or AA.

Sample Test Questions

1) Which of the following is NOT a part of planning?

     A) Setting goals
     B) Setting objectives
     C) Identifying ways to complete objectives
     D) Conducting meetings

The correct answer is D:) Conducting meetings. While conducting meetings is a part of a manager's role, it is not an official role under the planning category which consists of making departmental goals and objectives and determining how those objectives will be accomplished.

2) PERT is an acronym for what?

     A) Personal effort retention training
     B) Practical employment risk training
     C) Program evaluation and review technique
     D) Personnel employment round table

The correct answer is C:) Program evaluation and review technique.

3) Which of the following is NOT a part of a PERT chart?

     A) Optimistic time
     B) Pessimistic time
     C) Time expected
     D) None of the above

The correct answer is D:) None of the above. A PERT chart includes a most pessimistic time, a most optimistic time, time expected, and a most probable time.

4) What theory states "organizational change is inevitable and that organizations and people within the organizations have no other choice except following natural law"?

     A) The Mechanistic Theory
     B) Hierarchy of Needs Theory
     C) The Systems Theory
     D) Hawthorne Effect Theory

The correct answer is A:) The Mechanistic Theory.

5) Which of the following theories argues that the effect of studying something/someone changes the effects of the study?

    A) The Mechanistic Theory
    B) Hierarchy of Needs Theory
    C) The Systems Theory
    D) Hawthorne Effect Theory

The correct answer is D:) Hawthorne Effect Theory. This is when the interest in the people's problems affects the outcome, not the changes themselves.

6) Which of the following theories determines interdependence of variables?

    A) The Mechanistic Theory
    B) Hierarchy of Needs Theory
    C) The Systems Theory
    D) Hawthorne Effect Theory

The correct answer is C:) The Systems Theory. The Systems Theory deals with interdependence instead of independence of variables and their interactions. It started with a more intensive, very broad, wide-angle – involving a number of variables to measure complex inter-relationships – and inclusive viewpoint. Group behavior is seen in the system as broadly shaped and influenced.

7) Which is the second stage of Maslow's Hierarchy of Needs?

    A) Self-actualization
    B) Esteem needs
    C) Belonging and love
    D) Safety

The correct answer is D:) Safety. Safety is the second stage in Maslow's Hierarchy of Needs.

8) When something is measurable in number it is

    A) Naturalistic observation
    B) Qualitative
    C) Cross sectional studies
    D) Quantitative

The correct answer is D:) Quantitative. When something can be measured with numbers, like a completed number of surveys, it is considered quantitative.

9) Who is considered to be the father of modern management?

   A) Abraham Maslow
   B) Max Weber
   C) Chester Barnard
   D) Peter Drucker

The correct answer is D:) Peter Drucker. Peter Drucker is considered the father of Modern Management.

10) Who completed a study on the fastest and most efficient way to do a job?

   A) Frank Gilbreth
   B) Peter Drucker
   C) Max Weber
   D) Henry Gantt

The correct answer is A:) Frank Gilbreth. Frank and Lillian Gilbreth did a study on the most efficient way to do a job.

11) _____ is a way to show the time needed to complete a long or complicated project.

   A) PERT
   B) Critical Path Method
   C) Bar Chart
   D) Gantt Chart

The correct answer is D:) Gantt chart. A Gantt chart is used to show who will be working on or different stages of a project and the time each step takes.

12) Which person created the five management functions?

   A) Frank Gilbreth
   B) Peter Drucker
   C) Henri Fayol
   D) Max Weber

The correct answer is C:) Henri Fayol. Henri Fayol is credited with creating the five management functions which are (1) planning, (2) organizing, (3) commanding, (4) coordinating, and (5) controlling.

13) Controller our computer by clicking on pictures and menus means we are using a

    A) GIGO
    B) DOS
    C) GUI
    D) RAM

The correct answer is C:) GUI. GUI stands for graphical user interface.

14) LPC stands for

    A) Least personnel count
    B) Leverage people credentials
    C) Late potential credit
    D) Least preferred coworker

The correct answer is D:) Least preferred coworker. The LPC or least preferred co-worker is an important part of Fiedler's contingency theory.

15) Which of the following are the levels of management?

    A) Technical, interpersonal and conceptual
    B) Technical, interpersonal and line staff
    C) Training, managing, staffing
    D) Controlling, planning, retaining

The correct answer is A:) Technical, interpersonal and conceptual.

16) Your company participates in an Affirmative Action program. As a manager you interview two equally individuals for a new position. One candidate is white and one candidate is a pacific islander. What do you do?

    A) Hire the white candidate
    B) Hire the pacific islander candidate
    C) Hire neither and conduct more interviews
    D) Hire towards the quota determined by your HR department

The correct answer is D:) Hire towards the quota determined by your HR department. Affirmative Action programs are custom created for each organization in a certain geographic area. Affirmative Action gives minorities, including women, additional opportunities in the workforce.

17) Which of the following is considered a pioneer in management theory?

    A) Peter Drucker
    B) Mary Parker Follet
    C) Frank Gilbreth
    D) Henri Fayol

The correct answer is B:) Mary Parker Follet. This woman from the late 1800s wrote many books on management theory, and human relations. She also worked as a speaker and volunteer social worker.

18) Which of the following terms illustrates the order of authority in an organization?

    A) Flow chart
    B) PERT chart
    C) Chain of command
    D) Town hall

The correct answer is C:) Chain of command. The chain of command is a term that refers to who reports to who in an organization. An organizational chart would show this as well.

19) In Herzberg's Motivation-Hygiene theory, the Hygiene refers to what?

    A) Cleanliness
    B) Work environment
    C) Satisfiers
    D) Dissatisfiers

The correct answer is D:) Dissatisfiers. Herzberg's Motivation-Hygiene theory basically found what makes an employee satisfied. He called something that was a motivation a satisfier and anything that was a dissatisfier was referred to as hygiene.

20) When you find the answer to your problem but settle for something else is an example of the

    A) Implicit favorite model
    B) Bounded rationality model
    C) Econological model
    D) Morality model

The correct answer is B:) Bounded rationality model.

21) When you choose the solution that has the greatest benefit for you

    A) Implicit favorite model
    B) Bounded rationality model
    C) Econological model
    D) Morality model

The correct answer is C:) Econological model.

22) Which of the following people was associated with the Hawthorne Effect study?

    A) Peter Drucker
    B) Mary Parker Follet
    C) Elton Mayo
    D) Frank Gilbreth

The correct answer is C:) Elton Mayo. Elton Mayo is also considered the founder of the Human Relations Movement.

23) If you are an authoritarian, you ascribe to

    A) Theory X
    B) Theory Y
    C) Theory XY
    D) Management theory

The correct answer is A:) Theory X.

24) Which of the following is considered the father of strategic planning?

    A) Peter Drucker
    B) Chester Barnard
    C) Elton Mayo
    D) Frank Gilbreth

The correct answer is B:) Chester Barnard. Chester Barnard is considered the father of strategic planning.

25) Which of the following developed the acceptance theory?

    A) Peter Drucker
    B) Chester Barnard
    C) Elton Mayo
    D) Frank Gilbreth

The correct answer is B:) Chester Barnard. Chester Barnard felt that the authority did not reside on the person giving the orders, but in the minds and will of the subordinates that determined whether to accept or reject those order from above. If these four areas were met then the employee accepted the task or authority: 1) the employee must understand what is asked of them. 2) they agree that the task is in congruence with the goals of the organization. 3) they agreed that the task was in their own personal interest. 4) they were physically and mentally able to comply.

26) A manager who believes that all people are valuable and want to contribute to their best ability you ascribe to

    A) Theory X
    B) Theory Y
    C) Theory XY
    D) Management theory

The correct answer is B:) Theory Y.

27) Which of the following is NOT a contributor to an employee's attitude?

    A) Previous jobs
    B) Education
    C) Peers
    D) Family

The correct answer is B:) Education. Education is generally not considered a contributor to an employee's attitude.

28) When someone is producing at standard it is called

    A) Role
    B) Role conflict
    C) Norm
    D) Status

The correct answer is C:) Norm. A norm or status quo is considered standard.

29) Who created the contingency theory?

    A) Peter Drucker
    B) Chester Barnard
    C) Elton Mayo
    D) Fred Fiedler

The correct answer is D:) Fred Fiedler. Fred Fiedler created the contingency theory.

30) What standard is the following "Giving monetary values to realized sales"?

    A) Physical standard
    B) Capital standard
    C) Revenue standard
    D) Cost standard

The correct answer is C:) Revenue standard.

31) A company borrows $100,000 to fund the building of a house which they expect to sell for $150,000. However, the deal falls through and they can only sell it for $120,000. The result is a

    A) $120,000 gain
    B) $20,000 gain
    C) $30,000 loss
    D) $150,000 loss

The correct answer is C:) $30,000 loss. The $120,000 made less the $150,000 opportunity cost is $30,000.

32) The total value of the products a nation exports minus the total value of the products it imports over some period of time is

    A) The trade multiplier
    B) The trade surplus
    C) The balance of trade
    D) The trade deficit

The correct answer is C:) The balance of trade.

33) Which of the following is true of NAFTA?

    A) NAFTA works to solve trade disputes occurring between countries in different continents.
    B) As a part of NAFTA, Canada and the United States agree to help Mexico in trade matters.
    C) NAFTA works to lower trade barriers between the United States, Canada and Mexico.
    D) NAFTA is responsible for creating international accounting standards.

The correct answer is C:) NAFTA works to lower trade barriers between the United States, Canada and Mexico. Answers A, B and D are all incorrect. NAFTA created essentially a free trade zone between Canada, Mexico and the United States, but does not involve other countries.

34) Collective bargaining is

    A) When employees authorize unions to represent them all as one in negotiating with management.
    B) When employees all negotiate with management individually for the same benefits.
    C) When political parties negotiate with one another to decide the outcome of an election.
    D) None of the above

The correct answer is A:) When employees authorize unions to represent them all as one in negotiating with management. This is why employees join unions – to authorize them to represent them through collective bargaining.

35) Which of the following has the highest ranking when a company goes bankrupt?

    A) Preferred stock
    B) Anyone the company owes money to
    C) Common stock
    D) Bonds

The correct answer is B:) Anyone the company owes money to. Outstanding debts are one of the first things that get paid when a company goes bankrupt.

36) Who is the father of scientific management?

    A) Thomas Jefferson
    B) Steve Jobs
    C) Frederick Taylor
    D) Gordon Moore

The correct answer is C:) Frederick Taylor.

37) If net exports is negative than there is

    A) A favorable balance of trade
    B) A trade surplus
    C) An even balance of trade
    D) A trade deficit

The correct answer is D:) A trade deficit. In this case, a country exports less than it imports.

38) Which of the following is the most corrupt country?

    A) India
    B) Egypt
    C) Finland
    D) Somalia

The correct answer is D:) Somalia. Somalia and North Korea are currently tied for most corrupt according to the UN ranking scale.

39) What standard is the following "monetary value for the cost of operations, such as machine-hour-costs, cost of material per unit, cost of labor per unit, cost per unit of sales, etc."?

    A) Physical standard
    B) Capital standard
    C) Revenue standard
    D) Cost standard

The correct answer is D:) Cost standard.

40) Which of the following is a person who is present to facilitate discussion between groups, leading to a resolution of a problem?

    A) Mediator
    B) Negotiator
    C) Arbitrator
    D) Lawyer

The correct answer is A:) Mediator. Mediation involves a formal meeting and discussion between groups until an agreement can be reached. When mediation occurs, there is an individual called a mediator who is present to facilitate discussion.

41) What standard is the following "quantified standards at the operating level. Products produced in numbers, in value, material used in weightage and value, labor employed in house and in value, services rendered in value, etc."?

    A) Physical standard
    B) Capital standard
    C) Revenue standard
    D) Cost standard

The correct answer is A:) Physical standard.

42) Which of the following is NOT one of Henry Mintzberg's classifications of organizations?

    A) Simple
    B) Complex
    C) Organic
    D) Stable

The correct answer is C:) Organic. Henry Mintzberg classified organizations as either simple, complex, stable or dynamic.

43) A good TQM program does NOT include

    A) Determination of standards of quality
    B) Institution of an effective continuous on the job checking program with responsibilities and accountability firmly fixed
    C) A recording system for comparing errors vs. standards
    D) A method which provides alternatives to solutions

The correct answer is D:) A method which provides alternatives to solutions. A good TQM is made up of: (1) determination of standards of quality, (2) institution of an effective continuous on the job checking program with responsibilities and accountability firmly fixed, (3) a recording system for comparing errors vs. standards, (4) a method which spells out corrective action, and (5) to install a program of analysis and quality improvement whenever found needed.

44) Small businesses are assisted in getting loans by

    A) State governments
    B) Small Business Federal Loan Fund
    C) Large corporations
    D) Small Business Administration

The correct answer is D:) Small Business Administration. The SBA does not itself grant loans, but rather it backs them. This way, small businesses can get backed by the SBA and get a loan from a bank that the SBA partners with, making it easier than if they had to find the loans themselves.

45) Which of the following is NOT a way of measuring product mix?

    A) The number of product lines
    B) The number of individual products
    C) The number of product variations
    D) All of the above are measures of product mix

The correct answer is D:) All of the above are measures of product mix. Product mix can be measured in many different ways, including the number of product lines, individual products and product variations.

46) Which of the following statements is FALSE?

   A) A market supply graph will slope upward.
   B) A market demand graph will slope downward.
   C) The higher the price the higher demand.
   D) The higher the price the higher supply.

The correct answer is C:) The higher the price the higher demand. At higher prices people will be willing to buy less of a product, or fewer people will be willing to buy the product.

47) Showing a new employee how to run the machines and software that they will be using is called

   A) Vestibule training
   B) On the job training
   C) Orientation
   D) Initiation

The correct answer is B:) On the job training. They are trained with the actual equipment that they will be using.

48) Which of the following is NOT a protected Title VII class?

   A) Race
   B) Age
   C) Sexual preference
   D) Religion

The correct answer is C:) Sexual preference.

49) When a company sells many different products it is referred to as

   A) Product width
   B) Product variability
   C) Product mix
   D) Promotion

The correct answer is C:) Product mix. For example, a company that sells shampoo will most likely also sell conditioner, hair spray and a variety of other hair care products.

50) Which of the following is NOT an example of traditional authority?

A) Supervisor
B) Vice President
C) Bishop
D) Secretary

The correct answer is D:) Secretary.

51) Which of the following describes equilibrium price?

A) The highest possible price in the market at which companies can sell a single product.
B) The price which makes both consumers and suppliers happiest.
C) The price at which supply and demand cross on the graph, at which suppliers are willing to provide the amount that consumers are willing to purchase.
D) The lowest possible market price which will inherently result in the most products sold and therefore highest profits.

The correct answer is C:) The price at which supply and demand cross on the graph, at which suppliers are willing to provide the amount that consumers are willing to purchase. Although it is not the highest or lowest price, it does set the market in equilibrium.

52) Which of the following is responsible for ensuring employee safety?

A) OSHA
B) EEO
C) Department of Labor
D) COBRA

The correct answer is A:) OSHA.

53) Which of the following problem resolution options involves simple communication between groups?

A) Mediation
B) Negotiation
C) Arbitration
D) Litigation

The correct answer is B:) Negotiation. Negotiation is the least complicated of the methods and does not involve any third parties to discussion.

54) Which of the following is NOT a way to deal with risk?

  A) Assuming
  B) Avoiding
  C) Shifting
  D) Deflecting

The correct answer is D:) Deflecting.

55) Which of the following is an example of environmental stress?

  A) Construction noise
  B) Strong perfume
  C) Peers
  D) Broken heating unit

The correct answer is A:) Construction noise.

56) Which of the following people is considered the Father of Capitalism?

  A) Peter Drucker
  B) Adam Smith
  C) Elton Mayo
  D) Frank Gilbreth

The correct answer is B:) Adam Smith.

57) What is the main difference between stocks and bonds?

  A) Holders of stock are paid before holders of bonds when a company goes bankrupt.
  B) Holders of bonds have a creditor stake in the company and stockholders have an equity stake in the company.
  C) Holders of stock are guaranteed to receive face value after a specific amount of time.
  D) None of the above

The correct answer is B:) Holders of bonds have a creditor stake in the company and stockholders have an equity stake in the company. In other words, a bond is basically a loan and stock is buying a portion of the company.

58) Which of the following is an example of Maslow's first level of needs?

    A) Food
    B) Car
    C) School
    D) Church

The correct answer is A:) Food.

59) Giving a new employee a tour of the office space and introducing them to the people they will be working with is called

    A) Vestibule training
    B) On the job training
    C) Orientation
    D) Initiation

The correct answer is C:) Orientation. New employees will also often receive orientations during which they fill out necessary paperwork and are given a tour of their working environment. They will also be introduced to the people that they are working with and other necessary introduction activities.

60) Which is the second stage of Maslow's Hierarchy of Needs?

    A) Self-actualization
    B) Esteem needs
    C) Safety needs
    D) Physical needs

The correct answer is C:) Safety needs.

61) When you choose the best action for each situation

    A) Situational leadership
    B) Participative leadership
    C) Autocratic leadership
    D) Laissez faire leadership

The correct answer is A:) Situational leadership.

62) The purpose of the SBA is to

    A) Protect banks from the ill effects of bankruptcy of large companies
    B) Protect the interests of small families
    C) Protect the needs of small businesses
    D) All of the above

The correct answer is C:) Protect the needs of small businesses. The SBA is the Small Business Administration – a federal agency.

63) When a supervisor asks for opinions in making decisions

    A) Situational leadership
    B) Participative leadership
    C) Autocratic leadership
    D) Laissez faire leadership

The correct answer is B:) Participative leadership.

64) Which of the following is NOT part of the marketing mix?

    A) Product
    B) Price
    C) Plan
    D) Place

The correct answer is C:) Plan. The four P's which make up the marketing mix are product, price, place and promotion.

65) In a monopoly a product is

    A) Sold by only one company and there is no close substitute available.
    B) Sold by only a few companies, who have great influence over the market.
    C) Sold by hundreds of companies in competition with each other.
    D) Sold by one company, though there are many close substitutes available.

The correct answer is A:) Sold by only one company and there is no close substitute available.

66) Which of the following statements is FALSE?

A) Embargoes are always inclusive of all products and countries.
B) Embargoes are a legal form of trade restriction.
C) Embargoes are not considered an act of war.
D) None of the above

The correct answer is A:) Embargoes are always inclusive of all products and countries. Embargoes can be limited to certain products or can be all inclusive and targeted at specific countries.

67) Which of the following is a union function?

A) Negotiate pay
B) Creating new business policies
C) Budgeting
D) Creating statistical reports

The correct answer is A:) Negotiate pay.

68) When a company does a stock split they are

A) Mandatorily cutting the value of each stock in half without changing anything else.
B) Mandatorily doubling the value of each stock without changing anything else.
C) Cutting each stock in circulation into two stocks worth half the value.
D) Increasing the par value of the stock and decreasing the market value.

The correct answer is C:) Cutting each stock in circulation into two stocks worth half the value. This way the stock price goes down but the owners still hold the same value and the same share in the company.

69) CD-Rs offer which type of storage option?

A) Write Many Read Once
B) Write Once Read Many
C) Write Many Read Many
D) Write Once Read Once

The correct answer is B:) Write Once Read Many. This means that information can be stored on the disc only once and cannot be removed or rewritten. However, the disc can be viewed multiple times.

70) Moore's law relates to

    A) The amount of available technology
    B) The geographic dispersion of technology
    C) The number of different integrated circuits
    D) Data density

The correct answer is D:) Data density. In other words, the number of transistors per square inch.

71) The job which involves evaluating and assessing financial statements is

    A) Arbitration
    B) Leveraging
    C) Auditing
    D) Scientific management

The correct answer is C:) Auditing. Auditors are not employed by a company, but are hired by them to certify that financial statements are reasonable and accurate.

72) CD-ROMs store up to how many minutes of data?

    A) 50 minutes
    B) 80 minutes
    C) 100 minutes
    D) 120 minutes

The correct answer is C:) 100 minutes. This is the equivalent of 300,000 pages of text.

73) The price at which a stock is bought and sold is its

    A) Book value
    B) Par value
    C) EPS
    D) Market value

The correct answer is D:) Market value. Par value is the price that is actually stated on the stock and in the company record.

74) Which of the following is NOT true of CD-ROMs?

    A) They do not support audio or graphic data, only text
    B) They cannot be rewritten or erased
    C) They are often used in software distribution
    D) All of the above are true

The correct answer is A:) They do not support audio or graphic data, only text. CD-ROMs support both sound and visual data, along with textual data.

75) Which of the following e-commerce models describes when consumers post offers for goods or services online and business decide whether they wish to sell at the specified price?

    A) C2C
    B) B2C
    C) C2B
    D) B2B

The correct answer is C:) C2B. This is also called the consumer to business model.

76) A document which shows a companies expected cash payments and collections over a period of time is called the

    A) Balance Sheet
    B) Statement of Cash Flows
    C) Income Statement
    D) Financial Statement

The correct answer is B:) Statement of Cash Flows. Although it is not required that a company publish a statement of cash flows, it is often useful for them to consider cash flows and ensure that they have sufficient cash on hand to conduct day to day business.

77) Why is it necessary for companies to track information about cash flows?

    A) Because it is required by the government.
    B) Because it helps them to ensure that they have sufficient cash on hand to conduct day to day business.
    C) Because expenses and revenues do not necessarily coincide with cash flows.
    D) Both B and C

The correct answer is D:) Both B and C. Statements B and C are both correct, however statement A is incorrect because businesses are not required to have a statement of cash flows.

78) Liquidity is useful in measuring

A) The amount to which debt has been used in financing a business.
B) The ability of a company to cover its debts.
C) The amount of a company's assets which are necessary to daily operations.
D) The proportion of a company's revenues which go to paying expenses.

The correct answer is B:) The ability of a company to cover its debts. This is because it is effectively a measure of how much money they can come up with quickly.

79) What is the approximate annual savings of a 2/10, net 60 term?

A) 6%
B) 12%
C) 20%
D) 36%

The correct answer is B:) 12%. The savings would be 2%, with 6 payment periods per year.

80) The process of assessing and evaluating the integrity of financial statements and instituting measures to ensure their integrity is

A) Internal control
B) Auditing
C) Statement evaluation
D) Arbitration

The correct answer is A:) Internal control. Internal controls are important both to protect investors from dishonesty of management and to protect the company from dishonesty from employees.

81) Who owns the U.S. Federal Reserve Banking System?

A) The U.S. Government
B) Private shareholders of member banks
C) The Department of the Treasury
D) A consortium of international banks

The correct answer is B:) Private shareholders of member banks.

82) Auditors can analyze financial statements in an unbiased way because

    A) They are often intimately involved with the day to day management of the business.
    B) They are independent workers hired by the company and not employees.
    C) They are employees of a company but volunteer to help in auditing.
    D) None of the above

The correct answer is B:) They are independent workers hired by the company and not employees. Because they are not employees they are not affected by what the statements shows, and therefore have no reason to manipulate them to be more favorable.

83) Which of the following problem resolution options requires that both parties hire lawyers, and that binding decision is reached by judges and juries?

    A) Mediation
    B) Negotiation
    C) Arbitration
    D) Litigation

The correct answer is D:) Litigation. The results of litigation are legally binding.

84) Which of the following is an example of Maslow's third level of needs?

    A) Sex
    B) Money
    C) Love
    D) Home

The correct answer is C:) Love.

85) Breaking a large project down into smaller, easily completed jobs is

    A) Scientific management
    B) Balancing production
    C) Leveraging
    D) Moore's law

The correct answer is A:) Scientific management. Scientific management is a management style created by Frederick Taylor, which is basically like the assembly line system.

86) John Turner was laid off from his communications job. What law gave him the right to continue receiving health benefits by paying the monthly premium?

    A) OSHA
    B) ADA
    C) COBRA
    D) ERISA

The correct answer is C:) COBRA. The Comprehensive Omnibus Budget Reconciliation Act allows employees to retain medical insurance after they quit or are terminated, for up to 18 months.

87) When a country imports more than it exports it is referred to as a

    A) Balance of trade
    B) Trade surplus
    C) Trade deficit
    D) Equilibrium trade rate

The correct answer is C:) Trade deficit. This is an unfavorable balance of trade, whereas a trade surplus is a favorable balance of trade in which a country exports more than it imports.

88) Which of the following is NOT part of a training program?

    A) Job sharing
    B) Job rotating
    C) Temporary promotion
    D) Promotion

The correct answer is D:) Promotion.

89) Which of the following is an industry commonly known to have line employees?

    A) Automotive
    B) Woodworking
    C) Education
    D) Retail

The correct answer is A:) Automotive.

90) The Federal Trade Commission Act regulated which of the following

    A) Insider trading
    B) Employee safety
    C) Truth in advertising
    D) Retail sales

The correct answer is C:) Truth in advertising. The Federal Trade Commission Act of 1914 created the Federal Trade Commission and it dictated that advertising cannot be deceptive or unfair, and it must be backed up by evidence. This policy of honest advertising is referred to as truth in advertising. Later, the commission would invenstigate stock transactions.

91) Discounting options falls under the marketing mix category of

    A) Sales
    B) Product
    C) Price
    D) Promotions

The correct answer is C:) Price. Price describes the amount that the product is sold for. Examples of price decisions include discounting options, seasonal pricing and price strategy among others.

92) Which set of ISO certifications is concerned with environmental issues?

    A) 5000
    B) 9000
    C) 14000
    D) 20001

The correct answer is C:) 14000.

93) Hands off leadership is also called

    A) Situational leadership
    B) Participative leadership
    C) Autocratic leadership
    D) Laissez faire leadership

The correct answer is D:) Laissez faire leadership.

94) Which of the following tells employees and others what is the main purpose of the company is

   A) Vision
   B) Mission statement
   C) Company statement
   D) Business plan

The correct answer is B:) Mission statement.

95) Which of the following is the BEST example of an oligopoly?

   A) Potato farming
   B) Gas stations
   C) Restaurants
   D) Clothing

The correct answer is B:) Gas stations. As with cell phones, there are few small gas station companies. Most companies are large and they have great influence over each other's policies and prices.

96) A policy can be defined as a _____ action course that serves as a guide for the identified and accepted objectives and goals.

   A) Predefined
   B) Flexible
   C) Necessary
   D) Unknown

The correct answer is A:) Predefined.

97) Which of the following restricts unions?

   A) HIPPA
   B) WARN
   C) Taft Hartley Act
   D) ADA

The correct answer is C:) Taft Hartley Act. In 1947, Congress passed the Taft Hartley Act which outlawed for unions the closed shop, jurisdictional strikes, secondary boycotts and made additional requirements for unions.

98) A totalitarian leader

    A) Situational leadership
    B) Participative leadership
    C) Autocratic leadership
    D) Laissez faire leadership

The correct answer is C:) Autocratic leadership.

99) Kyle falls of the roof while doing his roofing job. What program will allow him to keep getting his wages while out of work?

    A) Lawsuit
    B) OSHA
    C) Health insurance
    D) Workers' compensation insurance

The correct answer is D:) Workers' compensation insurance. Workers' compensation insurance is required on the state or federal level for all business. This insurance pays worker's hospital bills and lost wages.

100) The intent of the Sarbanes-Oxley Act was to

    A) Help companies be better able to deal with the ethical problems raised by increased technology.
    B) Restore stakeholder confidence in the securities market after a series of scandals in the early 2000s.
    C) Create a commission that would monitor the accounting records of major businesses.
    D) Scare businesses into conforming with the GAAP standards in their accounting practices.

The correct answer is B:) Restore stakeholder confidence in the securities market after a series of scandals in the early 2000s.

101) Which of the following is the formula for determining net exports?

    A) Imports (Exports)
    B) Imports - Exports
    C) Exports/Imports
    D) Exports - Imports

The correct answer is D:) Exports - Imports. Net exports are also referred to as the balance of trade.

102) The way that people communicate with each other using their bodies

    A) Consideration
    B) Body language
    C) Communication
    D) Charisma

The correct answer is B:) Body language.

103) NAFTA stands for

    A) North American Free Trade Agreement
    B) North African Federal Truth Agreement
    C) North American Franchise Treatment Association
    D) North African Free Trade Association

The correct answer is A:) North American Free Trade Agreement. The agreement is signed between Mexico, Canada and the United States.

104) Brenda is paid piecework. If she is paid 75 cents for every hat she sows and she sows 15 in one hour, how much is she paid per hour?

    A) $7.50
    B) $8.50
    C) $9.75
    D) $11.25

The correct answer is D:) $11.25. Brenda is paid per piece. $.75 multiplied by 15 is $11.25 an hour.

105) When an employee receives an hourly wage and an extra bonus for each task completed it is called

    A) Salary
    B) Standard hour plan
    C) Commission
    D) None of the above

The correct answer is B:) Standard hour plan. When an employee receives an hourly wage and an extra bonus for each task completed they are on a standard hour plan.

106) Leadership characteristics that inspire employees is called

    A) Chain of command
    B) Vision
    C) Charisma
    D) Motivation

The correct answer is C:) Charisma.

107) Which of the following statements is NOT true about ISO certifications?

    A) The ISO charges a small fee to certify companies.
    B) The ISO 14000 certification sets forth guidelines for environmental management.
    C) One aspect of the ISO 9000 certification is that businesses have regular product quality evaluations.
    D) All of the above statements are true.

The correct answer is A:) The ISO charges a small fee to certify companies. The ISO itself doesn't certify companies, but rather independent organizations have been set up to do so.

108) Agreement of members of a group on a decision is called

    A) Consensus
    B) Group think
    C) Meetings
    D) Consideration

The correct answer is A:) Consensus.

109) What is the approximate annual savings of a 1/10, net 60 term?

    A) 6%
    B) 12%
    C) 20%
    D) 36%

The correct answer is A:) 6%. It's a 1% savings and there would be about 6 purchase periods in a year so the answer is (1%)(6) = 6%.

110) Leaders that use group ideas to make decisions

    A) Autocratic
    B) Laissez faire
    C) Democratic
    D) Trait

The correct answer is D:) Trait.

111) Which is NOT a factor that influences the favorableness of a leader?

    A) Leader-member relations
    B) Task structure
    C) Leader position power
    D) Charisma level

The correct answer is D:) Charisma level.

112) Labor unions operate on a basis of

    A) Franchise rights
    B) Collective bargaining
    C) Marketing mix
    D) Trade restrictions

The correct answer is B:) Collective bargaining. This is the idea that if all of the workers act as one in negotiating with management, then they will have more power in the negotiations than if a single worker were to attempt to negotiate with management.

113) When companies offer employees a portion of the money they save with increased productivity and efficiency it is called

    A) Profit sharing
    B) Franchising
    C) Gainsharing
    D) Reverse royalties

The correct answer is C:) Gainsharing. This is one way of giving employees incentives to work more efficiently.

114) Which of the following companies was NOT implicated in a scandal in the early 2000s?

A) Enron
B) Coca-Cola
C) Tyco International
D) All of the above were implicated in scandals

The correct answer is D:) All of the above were implicated in scandals. Due to the various different scandals occurring in the early 2000s, federal regulations concerning businesses were tightened. One example of this is the Sarbanes-Oxley Act.

115) ABC plant closes its offices and plant during a strike this is called a

A) Buyout
B) Strike
C) Arbitration
D) Lockout

The correct answer is D:) Lockout. A lockout is when an employer closes their plant or offices during a labor strike or union problem.

116) A billboard is an example of

A) Active listening
B) Two-way communication
C) One-way communication
D) None of the above

The correct answer is C:) One-way communication.

117) Which of the following incorrectly describes preferred stock?

A) Holders of preferred stock have voting rights.
B) Holders of preferred stock are guaranteed to receive dividends.
C) Holders of preferred stock are paid before holders of common stock.
D) Preferred stock is considered senior to common stock.

The correct answer is A:) Holders of preferred stock have voting rights. Holders of preferred stock typically do not have voting rights in a company, whereas holders of common stock do.

118) Leaders that give the group total freedom

   A) Autocratic
   B) Laissez faire
   C) Democratic
   D) Trait

The correct answer is B:) Laissez faire.

119) Which of the following is NOT a communication pattern?

   A) Chain
   B) Circle
   C) Wheel
   D) Arc

The correct answer is D:) Arc.

120) When someone receives too much information and cannot tell what is important from what is not it is called

   A) Overload
   B) Spam
   C) Decoding information
   D) Rejected information

The correct answer is A:) Overload.

121) The EEOC investigates violations of the

   A) WARN Act
   B) Kyoto Protocol
   C) Sarbanes-Oxley Act
   D) Civil Rights Act of 1964

The correct answer is D:) Civil Rights Act of 1964.

122) John is paid $1500 per computer he sells. This is his only compensation. This means he

   A) Is paid salary
   B) Is paid on commission
   C) Is paid piecework
   D) Is paid both salary and commission

The correct answer is B:) Is paid on commission. When a person is only paid a percentage or fixed amount based on the amount they sell, it is called commission only.

123) Which of the following would NOT be a good use for short term financing?

   A) Expanding the business
   B) Ease cash flow problems
   C) Temporary expenses
   D) None of the above

The correct answer is A:) Expanding the business. Expanding a company's operates would more appropriately be funded through long term financing.

124) When someone deliberately tampers with a message, leaving out information, it is called

   A) Overload
   B) Omitting
   C) Y pattern
   D) Highlighting

The correct answer is B:) Omitting.

125) The ability of an asset to be converted to cash is

   A) Leverage
   B) Financing ability
   C) Liquidity
   D) Usability

The correct answer is C:) Liquidity. The easier it is to convert an asset to cash, the more liquid it is.

126) Which of the following is NOT a supervisory function?

A) Marketing
B) Planning
C) Staffing
D) Organizing

The correct answer is A:) Marketing.

127) Which of the following is a commercial software which bundles together multiple interlinked applications?

A) Office Systems
B) Microsoft Office
C) Microsoft Corporation
D) CD-R

The correct answer is B:) Microsoft Office. Microsoft Office is sold by Microsoft Corporation.

128) Which of the following is an example of an extrinsic reward?

A) Raise
B) Self-esteem
C) Praise
D) Personal development

The correct answer is A:) Raise.

129) If a plant manager is tasked to reduce costs by 10% this is an example of what kind of goal?

A) Strategic
B) Long-term
C) Tactical
D) Operational

The correct answer is D:) Operational.

130) Which of the following is true for a year in which the purchases exceeded the overall sales of the firm?

A) The quantity of units in inventory decreases
B) A firm using FIFO will be concerned about potential reduction in taxes
C) A firm using LIFO will be concerned about potential reduction in taxes
D) A & B

The correct answer is C:) A firm using LIFO will be concerned about potential reduction in taxes.

131) Which of the following shows the relationship between employees and their peers?

A) Organizational chart
B) Gantt chart
C) Decision tree
D) Simulation

The correct answer is A:) Organizational chart.

132) Which of the following would NOT be a good use for long term financing?

A) Large construction projects
B) Expanding the company
C) Buying a new machine
D) None of the above

The correct answer is D:) None of the above. Long term financing would be the appropriate method for all of the options given.

133) Which of the following shows alternate paths for decision making?

A) Organizational chart
B) Gantt chart
C) Decision tree
D) Simulation

The correct answer is C:) Decision tree.

134) Opportunity cost is

A) The value of the best alternative not chosen.
B) The sum of the values of the alternatives not chosen.
C) The value of the worst alternative avoided.
D) The cost of choosing a particular option.

The correct answer is A:) The value of the best alternative not chosen. For example, if a company sells a car to someone for 20 thousand dollars, and could have sold it to a different person for 25 thousand dollars, the opportunity cost is 25 thousand dollars.

135) When a supervisor administers a questionnaire among participants that have never met it is called

A) Brainstorming
B) Sampling
C) Delphi technique
D) Groupthink

The correct answer is C:) Delphi technique.

136) With which of the following is a person guaranteed to be repaid face value after a certain amount of time?

A) Common stock
B) Preferred stock
C) Coupon
D) Bond

The correct answer is D:) Bond. Bonds are essentially a loan and the holder is guaranteed to get their money back in addition to receiving interest payments over time.

137) Trade restrictions are a(n)

A) Anomaly
B) Embargo
C) Reverse royalty
D) Trade deficit

The correct answer is B:) Embargo. Embargoes can be limited to certain products or can be all inclusive and targeted at specific countries.

138) Which of the following shows timelines for projects?

    A) Organizational chart
    B) Gantt chart
    C) Decision tree
    D) Simulation

The correct answer is B:) Gantt chart.

139) Who created Theory X and Theory Y?

    A) Max Weber
    B) Abraham Maslow
    C) Douglas McGregor
    D) Frank Gilbreth

The correct answer is C:) Douglas McGregor.

140) Which of the following deals with unions?

    A) NLRB
    B) FMLA
    C) TQM
    D) OSHA

The correct answer is A:) NLRB. The National Labor Relations Board is an independent federal agency to administer the National Labor Relations Act (NLRA), the primary law governing relations between unions and employers in the private sector.

141) Another name for main memory is

    A) Reusable memory
    B) Secondary storage
    C) Integrated circuitry
    D) Random Access Memory

The correct answer is D:) Random Access Memory. This memory is internal to the computer, quickly accessed and executed and is volatile.

142) This is a commission that investigates and prosecutes those business and individuals who discriminate against protected classes

   A) EEO
   B) OSHA
   C) FMLA
   D) ERISA

The correct answer is A:) EEO. EEO, Equal Employment Opportunity is a commission that investigates and prosecutes those business and individuals who discriminate against protected classes.

143) When two groups or individuals work together to resolve a problem it is called

   A) Negotiation
   B) Grievance
   C) Arbitration
   D) Mediation

The correct answer is A:) Negotiation.

144) Which of the following is NOT a possible internal control which a company could institute?

   A) Requiring that employees receive authorization before altering documents or removing them from the building.
   B) Dividing up duties among employees so that no single employee has the ability to manipulate financial statements for their own benefit.
   C) Hiring independent auditors to review financial statements and certify their reliability.
   D) All of the above are possible internal controls.

The correct answer is D:) All of the above are possible internal controls. Internal controls are designed to ensure that financial statements are accurate, which each of the options does.

145) The ISO 14000 classifications relate to a company creating a(n)

    A) Cash flow statement
    B) Information system management team
    C) System of ensuring stakeholder interests
    D) Environmental management system

The correct answer is D:) Environmental management system. The standards are a set of guidelines specifying how the business should go about creating and executing their EMS systems.

146) What is it called when a third party is facilitating negotiations?

    A) Concession
    B) Grievance
    C) Arbitration
    D) Mediation

The correct answer is D:) Mediation.

147) What is a third party person called to help resolve an issue between two parties?

    A) Mediator
    B) Negotiator
    C) Arbitrator
    D) Lawyer

The correct answer is C:) Arbitrator. With arbitration an impartial third party person is chosen to decide which of the groups is correct.

148) An employee that works on an assembly line performing the same task again and again is an example of

    A) Job specialization
    B) Job rotation
    C) Job sharing
    D) Job description

The correct answer is A:) Job specialization.

149) Two receptionists work at Widget, Inc., one in the morning and one in the afternoon. They are an example of

   A) Job specialization
   B) Job rotation
   C) Job sharing
   D) Job control

The correct answer is C:) Job sharing.

150) _____ is a federal law that sets minimum standards for most voluntarily established pension and health plans in private industry to provide protection for individuals in these plans.

   A) EEO
   B) OSHA
   C) FMLA
   D) ERISA

The correct answer is D:) ERISA. The Employee Retirement Income Security Act of 1974 (ERISA) is a federal law that sets minimum standards for most voluntarily established pension and health plans in private industry to provide protection for individuals in these plans.

151) When a person acts as expected as part of the group they are portraying their

   A) Role
   B) Groupthink
   C) Norm
   D) Status rank

The correct answer is A:) Role.

152) What is it called when a third party of empowered to resolve a disagreement it is called?

   A) Negotiation
   B) Grievance
   C) Arbitration
   D) Mediation

The correct answer is C:) Arbitration.

153) Which of the following is NOT true of main memory?

    A) It is an external form of data storage
    B) It is directly connected to the CPU
    C) It is volatile
    D) All of the above are true

The correct answer is A:) It is an external form of data storage. Main memory is internal, and it is directly connected to the CPU.

154) Who was a proponent of bureaucracy?

    A) Max Weber
    B) Abraham Maslow
    C) Douglas McGregor
    D) Frank Gilbreth

The correct answer is A:) Max Weber.

155) E-commerce is

    A) The buying and selling of goods and services over the internet.
    B) Conducting of business over the internet.
    C) The term used to describe online auction sites.
    D) None of the above

The correct answer is A:) The buying and selling of goods and services over the internet. E-commerce can consist of multiple different combinations of interactions between businesses and consumers.

156) Which of the following can NOT be discussed in a job interview?

    A) Education and degrees
    B) Children
    C) Previous wages
    D) Personality

The correct answer is B:) Children.

157) The grapevine of the organization is everything BUT

    A) Formal
    B) Generally accurate
    C) Verbal
    D) Exists in every organization

The correct answer is A:) Formal.

158) When a supervisor believes that all employees like work it is called

    A) Theory Y
    B) Theory X
    C) Hawthorne Effect
    D) TQM

The correct answer is A:) Theory Y.

159) _____ provides certain employees with up to 12 weeks of unpaid, job-protected leave per year.

    A) EEO
    B) OSHA
    C) FMLA
    D) ERISA

The correct answer is C:) FMLA. The Family and Medical Leave Act (FMLA) provides certain employees with up to 12 weeks of unpaid, job-protected leave per year.

160) Which set of ISO certifications addresses whether companies are looking after stakeholder interests?

    A) 5000
    B) 9000
    C) 14000
    D) 20001

The correct answer is B:) 9000.

161) A commercial agreement between an individual and the owner of a trademark is a

    A) Profit share
    B) Franchise
    C) Gainshare
    D) Reverse royalty

The correct answer is B:) Franchise. For example, many large fast food chains do not actually operate most of their locations. Individuals pay them in exchange for allowing them to use their name, logos and advertising.

162) This scientific study originally tested worker's output and light, later revealing unintended consequences

    A) Theory Y
    B) Theory X
    C) Hawthorne Effect
    D) TQM

The correct answer is C:) Hawthorne Effect.

163) Referent power is the same as

    A) Laissez faire leadership
    B) Charismatic leadership
    C) Peer pressure
    D) Expert leadership

The correct answer is B:) Charismatic leadership.

164) The Malcolm Baldrige National Quality Award is given for

    A) TQM
    B) Traditional leadership
    C) Performance excellence
    D) Expert leadership

The correct answer is C:) Performance excellence.

165) Regarding sexual harassment which of the following is NOT true

    A) Offenders can be same or opposite sex
    B) Victims do not have to be harassed personally but affected through environment
    C) Harasser must be a superior employee
    D) Harassment may occur without economic injury

The correct answer is C:) Harasser must be a superior employee.

166) Which of the following is NOT a part of Microsoft Office?

    A) PowerPoint
    B) Word
    C) Excel
    D) All of the above are part of Microsoft Office

The correct answer is D:) All of the above are a part of Microsoft Office. PowerPoint, Word and Excel are the most popular applications sold by Microsoft Corporation.

167) Who created a system of human needs and motivations?

    A) Max Weber
    B) Abraham Maslow
    C) Douglas McGregor
    D) Frank Gilbreth

The correct answer is B:) Abraham Maslow.

168) Long term success through customer satisfaction

    A) Theory Y
    B) Theory X
    C) Hawthorne Effect
    D) TQM

The correct answer is D:) TQM.

169) Who was responsible for developing the 14 principles of management?

  A) Max Weber
  B) Henri Fayol
  C) Douglas McGregor
  D) Frank Gilbreth

The correct answer is B:) Henri Fayol.

170) Which of the following are barriers to making decisions?

  A) Statistics
  B) Lack of statistics
  C) Emotions
  D) All of the above

The correct answer is D:) All of the above.

171) Which of the following is NOT a type of resistance?

  A) Logical
  B) Psychological
  C) Sociological
  D) Biological

The correct answer is D:) Biological.

172) The organizational structure where organizations are divided by products or divisions

  A) Functional
  B) Line and staff
  C) Product
  D) Matrix

The correct answer is C:) Product.

173) Who believed that managers make decisions based on their assumptions of human nature?

A) McGregor
B) Taylor
C) Ratter
D) Johnson

The correct answer is A:) McGregor.

174) When an interest in the people's problems affects the outcome, not the changes themselves, it is known as

A) Hawthorne effect
B) Taylor effect
C) Laissez faire effect
D) Groupthink effect

The correct answer is A:) Hawthorne effect.

175) Moore's law states that the number of transistors per square inch will double every

A) 6 months
B) 1 year
C) 18 months
D) 2 years

The correct answer is C:) 18 months. The original trend was that it doubled each year, however over time it has been amended to 18 months as the speed has slowed.

176) Factor that always stays the same

A) Dependent variable
B) Independent variable
C) Constant
D) Correlation

The correct answer is C:) Constant.

177) Which of the following is NOT a benefit of using CD-Rs to store information?

    A) They are easy to obtain and store
    B) They are relatively cheap
    C) They can store up to six hours of data
    D) All of the above are benefits of CD-Rs

The correct answer is C:) They can store up to six hours of data. CD-Rs can store only up to 80 minutes of data.

178) Information that is difficult to measure is called

    A) Quantitative
    B) Qualitative
    C) Longitudinal
    D) Dependent

The correct answer is B:) Qualitative.

179) If you believe that all people are good – you ascribe to this school of thought

    A) Biological
    B) Cognitive
    C) Structuralism
    D) Humanistic

The correct answer is D:) Humanistic.

180) Standards or principles

    A) Norms
    B) Values
    C) Rules
    D) Status quo

The correct answer is B:) Values.

181) Which of the following is NOT a factor with job satisfaction?

    A) Hours
    B) Pay
    C) Benefits
    D) Vacation location

The correct answer is D:) Vacation location.

182) When a person responds to a neutral stimulus _____ is being used.

    A) Classical conditioning
    B) Operant conditioning
    C) Extrinsic reinforcer
    D) Intrinsic reinforcer

The correct answer is A:) Classical conditioning.

183) Clayton Alderfer created his ERG theory based on the work of which theorist?

    A) Max Weber
    B) Henri Fayol
    C) Abraham Maslow
    D) Frank Gilbreth

The correct answer is C:) Abraham Maslow. Alderfer wanted to revise Maslow's Hierarchy of Needs to match empirical research.

184) When you are a secretary and there are seven levels between your role and the CEO, your organization is considered to be

    A) Fat
    B) Tall
    C) Flat
    D) Short

The correct answer is B:) Tall. A tall organization is one when the organizational chart is drawn out is tall.

185) A flat organization is an organization with

    A) A high ratio of mid level management to high level management positions.
    B) A low ratio of mid level management to low level employee positions.
    C) A low number (if any) of mid level management positions.
    D) A high ratio of low level employees to potential customers.

The correct answer is C:) A low number (if any) of mid level management positions. This way the top level management comes into direct contact with the low level employees.

186) Who first studied job motions with bricklayers, studying how fewer hand motions made the work faster?

    A) Max Weber
    B) Abraham Maslow
    C) Douglas McGregor
    D) Frank Gilbreth

The correct answer is D:) Frank Gilbreth.

187) In accounting, on a balance sheet, the assets are on the

    A) Left
    B) Right
    C) Both columns
    D) None of the above

The correct answer is A:) Left. A balance sheet is a financial statement that shows the assets (left) and the liabilities (on the right).

188) A neutral third party who helps resolve a conflict is known as a

    A) Mediator
    B) Negotiator
    C) Arbitrator
    D) Lawyer

The correct answer is A:) Mediator.

189) The UCC is best described as a/an

A) Law
B) Suggestion
C) Foundation for state law
D) Rules regulating inter-state sales

The correct answer is D:) Rules regulating inter-state sales.

190) Legitimate power is the same as

A) Laissez faire leadership
B) Traditional leadership
C) Peer pressure
D) Expert leadership

The correct answer is B:) Traditional leadership.

Test Taking Strategies

Here are some test-taking strategies that are specific to this test and to other DSST tests in general:

- Keep your eyes on the time. Pay attention to how much time you have left.

- Read the entire question and read all the answers. Many questions are not as hard to answer as they may seem. Sometimes, a difficult sounding question really only is asking you how to read an accompanying chart. Chart and graph questions are on most DANTES/DSST tests and should be an easy free point.

- If you don't know the answer immediately, the new computer-based testing lets you mark questions and come back to them later if you have time.

- Read the wording carefully. Some words can give you hints to the right answer. There are no exceptions to an answer when there are words in the question such as always, all or none. If one of the answer choices includes most or some of the right answers, but not all, then that is not the answer. Here is an example:

  The primary colors include all of the following:

  A) Red, Yellow, Blue, Green

  B) Red, Green, Yellow

  C) Red, Orange, Yellow

  D) Red, Yellow, Blue

  Although item A includes all the right answers, it also includes an incorrect answer, making it incorrect. If you didn't read it carefully, were in a hurry, or didn't know the material well, you might fall for this.

- Make a guess on a question that you do not know the answer to. There is no penalty for an incorrect answer. Eliminate the answer choices that you know are incorrect. For example, this will let your guess be a 1 in 3 chance instead.

What Your Score Means

Based on your score, you may, or may not, qualify for credit at your specific institution. The current ACE recommended score for this exam is 46. Your school may require a higher or lower score to receive credit. To find out what score you need for credit, you need to get that information from your school's website or academic advisor.

You lose no points for incorrect questions so make sure you answer each question. If you don't know, make an educated guess. On this particular test, you must answer 100 questions in 90 minutes.

Test Preparation

How much you need to study depends on your knowledge of a subject area. If you are interested in literature, took it in school, or enjoy reading then your study and preparation for the literature or humanities test will not need to be as intensive as that of someone who is new to literature.

This book is much different than the regular DSST study guides. This book actually teaches you the information that you need to know to pass the test. If you are particularly interested in an area, or feel that you want more information, do a quick search online. We've tried not to include too much depth in areas that are not as essential on the test. It is important to understand all major theories and concepts listed in the table of contents. It is also important to know any bolded words.

Don't worry if you do not understand or know a lot about the area. With minimal study, you can complete and pass the test.

We use test questions to teach you new information not covered in the study guide AND to test your knowledge of items you should already know from reading the text. If you don't know the answer to the test question, review the material. If it is new information, then this is an area that will be covered on the test but not in detail.

To prepare for the test, make a series of goals. Set aside a certain amount of time to review the information you have already studied and to learn additional material. Take notes as you study; it will help you learn the material. If you haven't done so already, download the study tips guide from the website and use it to start your study plan.

Legal Note

DSST is a registered trademark of The Thomson Corporation and its affiliated companies, and does not endorse this book.

FLASHCARDS

This section contains flashcards for you to use to further your understanding of the material and test yourself on important concepts, names or dates. Read the term or question then flip the page over to check the answer on the back. Keep in mind that this information may not be covered in the text of the study guide. Take your time to study the flashcards, you will need to know and understand these concepts to pass the test.

Management Theory: Empirical/Case Approach	**Management Theory: Interpersonal Behavior Approach**
Management Theory: Group Behavior Approach	**Management Theory: Cooperative Social Systems Approach**
Management Theory: Sociotechnical Systems Approach	**Management Theory: Decision Theory Approach**
Management Theory: Systems Approach	**Management Theory: Mathematical or Management Science Approach**

Understanding people and relationships. If people were understood perfectly, reaching organizational goals would not be difficult

The experience of past situations guide the present. Find out why an action succeeded or failed by analyzing the basic reasons

Propounded by Christian Barnard, it is the cooperative interaction of thoughts, ideas, wants and desires of two or more people

Work in groups rather than in isolation. The study of how behavior patterns in groups affect production

A manager's most important function is decision making and therefore decisions should be the central focus. All other functions of a manager are built around decisions

Credited to E.L. Trist, this approach seeks to emphasize the systems aspect of group behavior

Mathematical models forms part of this theory. Each situation is fraught in terms of available mathematical models and then analyzes the situation threadbare arriving at a mathematically correct decision

Management is a system, which envelops within itself many subsystems, all operating within the total environment

Management Theory: Contingency or Situational Approach

Management Theory: Managerial Roles Approach

Management Theory: Operational Approach

Economic Environment

Technological Environment

Social Environment

Political and Legal Environment

Ethical Environment

Propounded by Professor Henry Mintzberg. Observing what other mangers do, then using such observations as a platform for analyzing and concluding on the basis of such analysis

Any manager's performance is directly related to a set of given circumstance or contingency. Some theorist also feel that it takes into account not only situations but also on the behavior

Availability of capital, rate of interest, labor availability and how well things are organized, general price levels, the degree of productivity, the willingness of entrepreneurs and availability of managerial skills

Imparting knowledge from every other field of knowledge such as sociology, mathematics, economics, psychology etc.

Value systems unique to particular group of people or society. The value system consists of attitudes, behavior patterns, needs, wants, expectations, level of education, the degree of intelligence, general beliefs, customs and traditions

How good the available knowledge is used through technology is a factor to reckon with. How to conceive ideas, how to design, how to produce optimally, how to effect efficient distribution and how well marketing is done, are technology oriented

Holding on to moral principles of what is right and what is wrong, guided by value systems prevalent in society and generally behaving in a responsible way

Laws, rules, regulations, governmental polices that affect an organization

Social Responsibilities

Steps in Planning

Mechanistic Theory

Systems Theory

Revenue Standards

Frederick Taylor

PERT stands for what?

Self-actualization

Analysis of opportunities.
Setting of objectives.
Identify the basis. Compare
alternatives. Design relevant
plans. Quantify for control.

Organizations as well as mangers
should be socially responsive to the
society as a whole and should be
able to do their bit when a situation
calls for it

Organizational processes
should be guided and
influenced because all things
are interdependent

Organizational change
is inevitable and natural
processes should be allowed
to take their own course

Scientific management school

Giving monetary value to
realized sales

Highest need in Maslow's
hierarchy - Level 5

Program evaluation and
review technique

Esteem Needs	Belonging and Love
Safety	Physical Needs
Groupthink	Paradox
Synergy	Laissez-faire leader

Level 3 need

Level 4 need

Level 1 need

Level 2 need

Contradictory Conclusion

Conformity in a group situation

Hands off leadership

Cooperative action

Made in the USA
Middletown, DE
19 November 2020